How To WRITE A HIT SONG

▲ ▲ ▲

HOW TO WRITE A HIT SONG

The Complete Guide To Writing & Marketing Chart-Topping Lyrics & Music

By

MOLLY-ANN LEIKIN

Hit Songwriter
&
Songwriting
Consultant

HAL•LEONARD™

Published by
Hal Leonard Corporation
7777 West Bluemound Road
P.O. Box 13819
Milwaukee, WI 53213

Library of Congress Cataloging-in-Publication Data

Leikin, Molly-Ann.
  How to write a hit song

  1. Music, Popular (Songs, etc.) - Writing
and publishing. I. Title.
MT67.L35 1987 784'.028 87-2567
ISBN 0-8818-881-8 (formerly 0-399-513392-2
published by Putnam Publishing Group)

Printed in the United States of America

The author gratefully and alphabetically acknowledges the help and support of:

Brenda Andrews

Todd Brabec

Eugene Brissie

Celestial Seasonings Peppermint Tea

Judith Clair

Marcie Goodman

Harowitzim/Willmotzot

Ira Jaffe

Jay Morganstern

Chris Pepe

Wolfgang Puck's Four Cheeses Frozen Pizza

Mr. Rightstein

Ronny Schiff

Roger W. Scholl

Linda Seger

Paige Sober

Susan Terry

In memory of Leslie Earl Harowitz
who made it to the premiere after all.

CONTENTS

INTRODUCTION

I'm a hit songwriter. I have an Emmy nomination, gold records from Anne Murray and Placido Domingo and four ASCAP Country Music Awards. I wrote the themes and songs for twenty-eight television shows and movies, including "Eight Is Enough" and *Violet,* which won an Oscar. I was a staff writer for three major music publishers over a period of eight years and taught songwriting at UCLA.

My collaborators have included some of the best songwriters in the world: Charlie Black and Rory Burke, co-writers of "A Little Good News," sung by Anne Murray; Steve Dorff, composer of "Through the Years," sung by Kenny Rogers; Jerry Crutchfield, who wrote "Two Steps Forward and Three Steps Back" with me, had numerous hits with other writers, and is Lee Greenwood's producer; and Lee Holdridge, a master film composer.

I remember when I used to dream of being a hit songwriter. I wrote all day and rewrote all night. I ached to hear my songs on the air and wanted nothing else. In spite of the mocking voices telling me the odds were too great and I'd never make it, something kept urging me on. Someday, I knew I'd get what I was after.

And I did.

People have asked me repeatedly if I'm from a musical family. I have to answer this way. My paternal grandfather Louis Leikin was born in Russia at a time when young men were drafted into the army. So when male babies were born, their births were not registered. My grandfather was fifteen when the government finally caught up with him. Arriving for his physical, he told the authorities he was a virtuoso violinist and should be in the army orchestra.

Unfortunately, on audition day, Grampa Louie appeared with his arm in a sling but was so passionate in convincing the army of his virtuosity, they accepted him without an audition.

A few weeks later, the orchestra was touring near the Polish border. Removing his cast and leaving behind the violin he never *did* know how to play, Grampa Louie escaped. So if you ask me if I'm from a musical family, I'd have to say not really . . .

The closest I came to having a relative even remotely connected to show business was my Uncle Harold, who was really in the meat business but who gave the farm report every weekday at 6 A.M. on the country station in Ottawa, Canada.

I became a hit songwriter because I wanted to be one. I was driven. I would accept nothing less. I had to do this or die. If *you* have that same fire burning in you, read on and I'll show you how I did it—how the pros do it—and how *you* can do it, too.

As a songwriting consultant in Santa Monica, California, I work with clients of all ages and levels of musical and lyrical ability. I'm proud to tell you that some of my clients have their songs on the air right now. One was nominated for a Grammy. Maybe next year at this time it'll be your turn. My clients know that consulting with me is as important to their success as that new synthesizer or mixing board, because without a great song, all the technical wizardry available to them is meaningless. A hit song can earn its writer and publisher $100,000 in royalties each year, *every* year, for the rest of their lives. Somebody has to write the hits. It might as well be you.

PREFACE

Songwriting is the most glorious and terrible thing I know. It is the former when I'm smitten with a magical idea, and I'm happy to let it keep me awake all night. The thunder pumping through my veins stimulates me to stretch my abilities, to struggle to perfect and pamper my new song like a beloved child.

Then there are days when I'm stuck on a particular song, or when everybody seems to reject what I've written and I feel as inconsequential as a wad of dirty chewing gum someone's trying to scrape off his Gucci shoe. As devastating as it feels, and as hard as I may fall, somehow I always forget the negative side of songwriting the next time I get an idea. The thunder starts pumping again. I pick up my pen, and I'm home.

Writing makes me feel whole and substantial in a way nothing else does. When I hear my songs on the radio and see them listed on the charts, I feel a great sense of triumph. As for the songs that are still in the drawer and never made it to the radio, I cherish them, too, and maybe even love them a little more. The awards on my walls remind me that I made the right choices after all at the crossroads of my life, where I walked right by the signs pointing to the safe, familiar places and headed instead into the uncharted forests, singing.

SONG STRUCTURE— THE LYRIC

Some of you write words and music. Some write only lyrics and others compose only melodies. But to be successful songwriters, it's important for you to know how to structure the whole song, not just the part you create. So if you're a composer, don't skip over the chapter on lyrics. And lyricists, pay close attention to the chapter on melody. You may think you don't need to know it, but you *do*. Someday your collaborator may be stuck and will need your help.

THE LYRIC

A hit song is usually less than two and a half minutes long. Every hit— whether it was written by Stephen Foster, Stephen Sondheim, or Stevie Wonder—has a specific structure, a musical and lyrical pattern that repeats.

A hit song has to have focus. We need to know immediately what it is about. Each line of lyric in your song has to relate to the title. It should add something to embellish and enhance our understanding of the subject matter. If you were writing a song about shoes, you'd include ideas about laces, patent leather, sneakers, cowboy boots, soles, scuffs, worn-down heels, sizes, corns, bunions, high heels, etc. You wouldn't suddenly throw in something about a lawn mower unless the shoe was mutilated by one.

So when deciding what to write about, find a theme and tell yourself what the song is going to be about in the first line. Stick to that narrative theme all the way through to the end. If you were watching a movie about a boxer who gets a shot at the title, nearly every scene and line of dialogue in that story would have to do with the man's quest for victory. The film wouldn't wander off and start telling a different story. It would remain focused on its original theme. Your songs have to be focused, too.

Exercise

Take a clean sheet of paper. Write the words "little red schoolhouse" at the top. Then list every picture or feeling those words evoke in you. Ask yourself fifty to a hundred questions like these:

1. Is the school old or new?
2. In what state is it located?
3. Is it in the country or the city?
4. How big is it?
5. Does it need paint? If so, where?
6. What season is it?
7. Is there a weathervane?
8. Is there a bell? What kind?
9. Is the school on a hill?
10. What century is it?
11. What time of day is it?
12. Are there any animals nearby? If so, what kind?
13. Are there any flowers and trees? If so, what kind and what color?
14. Are there steps into the school?
15. Are there children outside?
16. What are the children doing?
17. What are the children wearing? Describe every detail of their appearance—from haircuts to frayed collars to shoe laces.
18. How old are the children?
19. Are they happy? If not, why not?
20. What is remarkable about the sky above the school?
21. What kind of desks are inside? Are they new?
22. If not, is anything carved on them?
23. Do you hear anything? Smell anything?
24. Is the teacher old or young? A man or a woman?

You could continue listing information about this little red school-house for hours, creating a picture, embellishing it, refining it. Your picture has colors in it, which heightens the impact because it's easier to visualize. I chose the concept of a little red schoolhouse because every-one has seen one, whether it was on television, in the movies, or in real life. Each of us sees a different picture, based on personal experience and imagination. And everybody can list the details of what their par-ticular little red schoolhouse looks like. Most of my clients say the building is similar to the one they saw on the television show "Little House on the Prairie." But one client, who is from New York City, said that his little red schoolhouse was in Greenwich Village. Two brothers said the teacher was a very strict nun, while my next client that day told me the teacher was a handsome young man with a beard. It doesn't matter that we see the picture differently, as long as we see something. And we do.

If you were going to write a song about this little red schoolhouse, you would choose the information you wanted to use from the long list of possibilities you've just created as a resource for yourself. You're not just sitting with a blank page trying to squeeze something out of your brain. You have a lot of choices of ideas, feelings and pictures to include in your song from the research you've just done. And that's half the work completed right there.

I do this exercise with all my new clients. It's an excellent way of showing them how to organize their thoughts. It proves to my clients who claim to be unable to write lyrics or think they aren't capable of writing visually, that they *are,* particularly if they start with a strong title, preferably one with a picture in it. This exercise shows lyricists how to keep digging for more information and make their images as specific and detailed as possible. To me, songs are *ear paintings,* and you have to make them vivid. This is the decade of dazzle. There are lots of distractions for your audience. If you want to "hook" a listener, build irresistibility into your songs.

When you have an idea for a new song, do the exercise just as you did with "little red schoolhouse." List everything that's pertinent and col-lect information by asking yourself fifty to a hundred questions about the song. If you can't list anything that goes with your idea, the chances are you either haven't thought it through carefully enough or your subject isn't big enough to warrant a whole song.

All songs have at least two distinct lyrical and musical sections, called A and B sections, that are repeated at least once. The most common contemporary hit song form is the ABAB form. The other is the AABAB form, and will be dealt with later in this chapter. All contemporary songs are structured in this way or use variations of one or the other of these forms. "Maybe It Was Memphis", by Michael Anderson is ABAB.

MAYBE IT WAS MEMPHIS
(by Michael Anderson)

Lookin' at you through a misty moonlight
Katydid sing like a symphony
Porch swing swayin' like a Tennessee lullaby
Melody blowin' through the willow tree
What was I s'posed to do? Standin' there lookin' at you
Lonely boy far from home

Chorus:
Maybe it was Memphis, maybe it was Southern summer nights
Maybe it was you, maybe it was me
But it sure felt right.
Maybe it was Memphis, maybe it was Southern summer nights
Maybe it was you, maybe it was me
But it sure felt right.

Read about you in a Faulkner novel
Met you once in a Williams play
Heard about you in a country love song
Summer night beauty took my breath away
What was I s'posed to do? Standin' there lookin' at you
Lonely boy far from home

Chorus:

Ev'ry night now since I've been back home,
Lie awake driftin' in my memory
Think about you on my mama's front porch swing
Talkin' that way so soft to me
What was I s'posed to do? Standin' there, lookin' at you
Lonely boy far from home

Chorus:

The A section is the verse, the B section is the chorus. The lyric in the A section is different in each verse, while the lyric in the B section remains the same all the way through. Sometimes songs have a third or C section, which is called the bridge, and is only played once. This song does not have a bridge, so obviously, not all songs need one. We'll discuss bridges in the chapter on melody.

The title in this lyric falls right at the beginning of the chorus. That's usually the best place to put it. Sometimes titles appear in the last lines of the chorus or somewhere else in the body of the song, but as beginners, it's helpful structurally to plan on putting your titles at the beginning of the chorus and build your songs around them.

You'll notice the title, "Maybe It Was Memphis", is repeated at the beginning of the fourth line of the chorus lyric. Since each chorus contains the title twice, by the time the song has played all the way through, the title has been sung twelve times. That may seem too repetitious. And sometimes it is. I'm not saying you <u>must</u> repeat your titles twelve times in every song, but you should use this song as a model of a lyric that truly works. When customers walk into record stores, they ask for the songs they want by title. By repeating the title, you're making it easier to remember the name of your song.

Now that you know where to place the title and have seen the physical appearance of this hit lyric, it's important to feel how the *rhythm* changes from the verse to the chorus. When you snap your fingers or tap your toe in time with a song, you're feeling its rhythm. The rhythm of "<u>looking</u>' at <u>you</u> through a <u>misty</u> <u>moon</u>light/<u>katy</u>did <u>singin</u>' like a <u>symphony</u>" is consistent throughout the verse. There are four stressed syllables (underlined) in each line. We are almost mesmerized by the repetitious rhythm or meter of the verse. But when the chorus begins, the rhythm changes drastically and startles us. The title is six syllables, and since the change in rhythm is so startling and strong, it surprises us and makes us pay attention. It is supposed to.

The title is the lyric half of "the hook". Every hit song must have a hook. By definition, the hook is the part of the song that draws you in and keeps you listening. *It is the strongest line of lyric sung on top of the strongest line of melody.* When you find yourself singing in the shower, you're singing the hook. What's even more surprising, you may not have realized you even liked the song you're singing. You may whistle a tune while you make the coffee or repair the garden gate. You're whistling the hook. I've often awakened in the morning with a song running through my head. The part of the song I'm hearing is the hook. I know you've had that experience, too. The part of the song that first springs out of the subconscious is the hook.

Now that you understand what a lyric hook is, be aware that the music has to have hooks, too. Without them, nobody will ever notice or hear your work. And besides being vehicles for us to express ourselves, songs serve as a way for us to share our feelings with our audience. In order to insure ourselves of having an audience, we have to hook them.

Beginning songwriters often fall into the trap of making their work too symmetrical. They feel that if the first line of a song has eight beats, each of the following lines has to match. They don't. It would make your lyric much more interesting to have the lines vary in length. Try a verse with lines of three, nine, seven and two syllables. You'll surprise yourself at how interesting the rhythm will be. Verses don't have to be just four lines long. They can be five or five and a half or even just three. The only thing I do recommend is they time out to twenty-five seconds or less, no matter how many lines you write. Remember, a song is not a novel.

If you're writing a lyric first and are then going to find a composer to write music for it, changing the meter by varying the lengths of the lines will help your musical partner to create something that is melodically *unpredictable*. The fewer the beats lyrically, the greater the chance the composer has to create a memorable melody.

"Maybe It Was Memphis" is an intriguing title. The city name makes it sound a little exotic, and the alliteration of the m's make it fun to sing. What makes this lyric sizzle are the images it contains, and the references to literature. It is intelligent, articulate and original. As an exercise, read this lyric again and make a list of all the pictures or images you see, such as "Katydid singin', porch swing swayin', melody blowin' through a willow tree". One picture suggests a hundred others, as we've seen from the little red schoolhouse exercise. A song with pictures in it appeals to two senses - sound and sight - thereby creating a second level of involvement for the audience. The reason I specifically chose this lyric is because the images Michael Anderson used are romantic and haven't been used before. As listeners, when we experience this song, we are taken on a two and a half minute adventure to places most of us have never been, where the moon is all misty, Katydids sing, porch swings sway and a young woman is seduced by a man who is like a character in a Faulkner novel or a Tennessee Williams play. That's good writing. We aren't just missing you, kissing you, ooh ooh, baby, oh yeah, which is where so many dull lyrics lead us these days. It's unusual for a lyric to contain as many images and literary references as "Maybe It Was Memphis" does, and yours certainly don't have to be this visual on your first time out, but every time I hear this song, I see and feel something new. That keeps me *interested*. Keep your audience interested, too, when writing your lyrics.

From here on, whenever you listen to songs on the car radio or on the stereo at home, try to imagine the lyrics being typed across a page by a computer - one line on the page for each line of lyric. In the case of "Maybe It Was Memphis", you will see six lines of alternating lengths of lyric in the verse and another six lines in the chorus. Listen to "see" where the title comes. If you train yourself to hear a song this way, you can automatically teach yourself to study the structure of every song you hear. It will prove to you how every hit has a simple and basic shape, which is just like a floor plan. The art takes over once that plan is made.

LISTEN TO THE COLORS

In my first songwriting workshop, the instructor underlined each single rhyme (joke, Coke) in red, each double rhyme (jingle, mingle) in green, each triple rhyme (banana, Havana) in blue. He circled all the picture words (Porsche, goat) in yellow. Intense feelings were circled in orange. His theory was the more colorful and illegible the lyric after you went through it with your crayons, the better. If you just have a series of red underlines and your song doesn't feel or sound terrific yet, perhaps you need to add color - a picture or a double rhyme. I like to shoot for at least three colors in each song.

Exercise

As an exercise, write a new lyric to the melody of "Maybe It Was Memphis". Choose a subject that is completely different. (One of my clients called her song "Harry On A Harley"). Put your title at the beginning of the chorus. You don't have to restrict your title to just six syllables, but try to keep it to seven. I'm sure you remember the TV show "Name That Tune." There was a segment called "Bid a Note." The contestants would say "I can name that tune in seven notes." Then six. Then five. And you could actually recognize the melody in those few notes. The reason was the band was playing the *title* line.

As you do your exercise, put one syllable of your lyric where each syllable of lyric is in the existing song. Try not to add any beats or your lyric will feel crowded and won't "sing" well. Stay as close to the original plan as possible. Remember, you're used to Michael Anderson's lyric, so allow yourself some distance and give your own idea time to develop. Write about whatever feels appropriate to accompany the music. One piece of advice, though: the most lasting and remunerative songs are *love songs*.

When you have a draft of your new lyric, sing it to the melody of "Maybe It Was Memphis". Be sure you don't put the em*pha*sis on the wrong syl*lab*le. Keep the accents and the language as natural as if you were speaking to someone.

Don't compete with Michael for greatness. Just do the exercise the best you can. If you're stuck for an idea, try writing something funny. It worked for my client when he wrote "Harry on a Harley", and the sequel, "Linda in a Lexus". It'll work for you, too. By going for humor instead of emotional intensity, there won't seem to be as great a demand on you, so the exercise will be fun. And I feel writing should always be fun.

If you've only got one verse and a chorus, that's okay. If you've only got one line, that's okay, too. If you only have a feeling about what you think the song is saying to you, that's a beginning.

The main thing is to get started and to stroke yourself, giving yourself permission to proceed. Your first songs won't be brilliant, so make peace with that. And be prepared to write your verses and choruses over and over again. Maybe even fifty times. That's normal. Songs don't usually arrive in whole chunks. They often come out a phrase at a time. Your first lyric might take a week or a month to finish. But that's normal, too.

I remember my first visit to the British Museum. I'd been studying literature and assumed Shakespeare, Keats, Shelley and the guys sat down at their desks and wrote whole, perfect poetry right off the top of their heads. I can't tell you how gratifying it was to see early drafts of their work with words and whole lines crossed out in the display cases.

CLICHÉ CONTROL

There is a tendency among all developing writers to use clichés - phrases we've heard over and over again in songs but which shouldn't be there. "I'm on the shelf", "I'm blue", and "morning light" are the phrases that come immediately to mind and cause the same negative response in me as chalk scratching on a blackboard. The true test of whether a word or phrase should be in a lyric is *not* whether you can get away with it because somebody famous did, but *if you're saying something new* and it sounds as natural as your conversation.

Like most writers, I've felt alone a lot in my life, and I've expressed that isolation in a thousand ways. But I've never *said* "I'm on the shelf". That is an expression that was acceptable in the forties and may still be lurking around, but *only* because it rhymes with "self" and nothing else does. However, just because a word rhymes is no good reason to use it. It has to say exactly what you mean. I've never used the phrase and none of my successful colleagues have, either. Therefore, it doesn't belong in our songs. If you want to say you've been by yourself and make it rhyme, try working with "I've been alone" instead. That sounds much more natural and leaves you many more choices for rhymes. So get off your shelves and write in the vernacular.

Like many writers, I'm moody, and when I've been unhappy I've told my friends "I'm depressed", "I'm bummed", "I'm down." But I've never said "I'm blue." That, too, is a dated cliché. We're writing songs for now, so our lyrics have to sound contemporary. I've heard some wonderful, seductive lines in my time, but no man has ever asked me to stay with him 'til the "morning light". I've heard, "I want you to stay here all night" or "please don't go home 'til tomorrow," but I've never heard this "morning light" phrase anywhere except in a bad lyric. Leikin's first law is, sing it the way you say it. If you wouldn't say it, don't sing it, either.

For your very own bottle of Cliché Control spray, write to me at the address in the back of this book. Please include $1.00 (U.S.) for postage.

THE MELODY

The lead sheet for "Maybe It Was Memphis" is included in this chapter. If you read music, you'll find it helpful in understanding the structure of melody. If you don't read music, buy the record. If you can't find it, I'm sure you will remember it, since it was on the air once an hour for three or four months.

In constructing a melody, there are several general guidelines to follow. Then inspiration should take over from there. Most hit songs are 32 bars long. A bar is the popular name for measure, which is enclosed between vertical lines on the music staff, and indicates a regular, prescribed number of beats. You can see from the accompanying lead sheet that the first measure or bar of "Maybe It Was Memphis" starts with "lookin'" and ends with "light". "Maybe It Was Memphis" is written in 4/4 time, meaning there are four beats in each bar. (The top figure tells the number of beats in the measure; the bottom indicates what kind of note gets a beat - in this case, a quarter note. In 2/4 time, there are two beats in a measure, with the quarter note again getting one beat. In 2/2 time, it is the half note that gets one beat.)

Some songs have 31 bars, some 33, because while they follow the guidelines of form, they aren't stuck in it. Music *is* an art, after all. But no matter how many bars you have in your song, you should get to the hook within twenty-five seconds. So keep your introduction short - maybe as few as two bars. The introduction is the instrumental section that begins the song. The song doesn't officially start until the verse melody and the lyric come in. Often writers who are in love with the power of their synthesizers go on for as many as sixteen bars of intro before beginning the actual song. Don't. Four is plenty. Two is better. You've got to hook your audience fast. They'll only give you a few seconds and then move on to something else that grabs them more easily. So don't lose them in a long, repetitive intro.

In trying to understand why it's so important to hook an audience quickly, consider commercials and jingles. Their purpose is to sell you a product in twenty seconds. Now they're shortening the length of commercial spots to fifteen seconds, so the message has to be even more compact. The same holds true for melodies. You only get a few seconds to interest your audience in your product. So don't expect anyone to sit patiently waiting for something to happen. *Make* it happen early.

After the title, the melody is the most important part of the song. Lyricists might be upset hearing this, but it is the truth. Make peace with that. The melody is the first thing we hear. If we like it, we'll stay tuned. We respond in a very open, natural, subjective state - like babies. I know you've seen toddlers dancing and singing to music when you know they don't understand a syllable of the lyric. The toddler test is really a good way to judge the merits of a tune, especially an up-tempo or rhythmic one.

When we hear a melody, we either like it or we don't. If we do like the tune, it usually isn't until we've heard it several times that we finally hear the lyric. You can have a brilliant lyric, but if it has a weak melody, nobody will ever hear any of it because the melody hasn't done its job. *The function of the melody is to reach out and grab us in an unguarded, primitive, totally emotional state and hold our attention long enough for the more civilized and intellectual lyric to take hold and give us some words to sing.* Don't expect the lyric to do the melody's job.

The music of the verse shouldn't be any longer than twenty-five seconds. Tops. Before a recent seminar I gave for songwriters in Texas, I studied two Babyface songs recorded by Grammy winner Toni Braxton that are on the current Hot 100 <u>Billboard</u> chart, and found drastic rhythmic and melodic changes occurring in the verses at twelve-second intervals. That's what you're competing with, so don't dismiss these songs as trivial or accidental. They're not. They're the industry standard. So make sure your melodies are interesting and "hooky" enough to compete with what you hear on the radio.

Whatever you do melodically, keep your audience *surprised*. If the tune is too predictable, you'll lose everybody. Fast. And once they go, they're gone forever. Remember - you need *magic* in your melodies. You're not just writing music by the pound.

The range of most pop singers is an octave and a third - middle C to the E in the octave above it. An octave is eight notes - the musical distance, for example, from Middle C to the C just above it. If you write a song with a range greater than an octave and three notes, you'll be hard-pressed to find a singer with the ability or "chops" to handle it. My song, "An American Hymn", has a range of an octave and five. I didn't write the melody, but thank God for Placido Domingo, who recorded it. I doubt anybody else could have hit the high notes, and then I would be minus a platinum record. In your writing, don't count on the Domingo's to save you. As beautiful as "An American Hymn" is, nobody else has ever sung it as far as my ASCAP statements show. That's a shame, since the song is one of my best. But the truth is, no singer will record anything that shows his/her voice to be less than perfect.

Remember, too, that all hit melodies change dramatically from the verse to the chorus. At that break, there is a rhythm change as well as a melodic one.

Most hit "power" ballads, such as Dolly Parton's "I Will Always Love You", end their verses on lower notes than the ones on which the chorus starts. As a rule, to create tension and drama in a melody, always go up into the chorus, not down. The most effective jump is a major third - C to E, for example. More and more these days, rock songs break the rule of going up, but you can be sure the rhythmic hooks at the beginning of the choruses are strong enough to overcome the melody's drop in intensity, and keep us listening.

Most people are more comfortable writing lyrics than music, because we speak words and we write words. We use words all the time, so we practice daily. But we don't speak music. That's okay. Music is something we *feel*, something we hear inside our heads and in our hearts. And we feel all the time. So don't be intimidated by your clumsy musicianship or your inability to read music or even play an instrument. Many of the world's greatest musicians never write original songs, they just interpret what other people have already written. So don't feel you have to be a great keyboard player or guitarist to write a great melody. Having some musical "chops" would certainly help you create melodies, but it isn't mandatory. If you hear a tune inside your head, you can whistle it into a tape recorder and then hire a musical secretary or arranger to embellish it with chords. *The melody is just a series of single notes you can hum or sing in the shower.* There aren't any chords or arrangements involved in its conception.

The best songwriters I know feel their songs first and then sit down at their instruments to embellish them. For most songwriters, writing music is not a matter of deciding about quarter notes and staccato sixteenths and minor thirds. It is simply a process of turning their feelings into music. If you feel something deeply and it causes you to stop in the middle of the day and race to the piano or pick up the guitar, what is happening is that your feelings and thoughts are traveling to your fingertips and coming out as a single line melody. I suggest you keep a cassette recorder running at all times when you write, so you don't have to worry about remembering what you write. Then, if you find a line of melody you love, you can just rewind the tape.

When new clients come to me, they often have weak, predictable melodies and ask me to suggest chord progressions that will make their music more interesting. The truth is no chord pattern can strengthen a weak tune. If a composer has gotten into a hole melodically, it's because he/she is not writing *pure* melody. They're relying on the chords to create the tune for them. Don't do that. Write the simple melodic line first and *then* go find the chords that enhance it.

Contrary to whatever you've seen romanticized and fantasized in movies, most contemporary writers do not "write" their songs on staff paper while the songs are being created. The composers get their melodies down on tape and then either write out the melody on staff paper later or take the tape to a music copyist who does that for them. The act of writing a melody is really just creating the music. The notation is usually done later.

Once you have a melody line that you like, one that's catchy and doesn't sound like anything else you've ever heard, decide which part of the song it is. See what goes with it, just as if you were coordinating your wardrobe. You wouldn't use two shades of red that clash. Be sure your music doesn't either.

If you've got the first line of the chorus, finish the melody to the whole chorus and then work backwards to create a verse melody that leads up to the first line of the chorus. It's always helpful to write the chorus first, just as with the lyric, because everything has to relate back to it. Otherwise, you're just writing blind. If the line of melody you've writen feels like a verse, then you know you should be building on that line musically and emotionally to lead up to the chorus, which is the high point of the song.

Just as each lyrical phrase should relate to the title, every musical phrase should also relate to the title line musically. It should all belong in the same song. The famous four notes of Beethoven's Fifth wouldn't blend well or belong in the same verse as the title line of "I'm Dreaming of a White Christmas", right? And the chorus of "End of the Road" wouldn't go with "The Star Spangled Banner". So make sure the feeling and texture of the music is consistent but interesting and full of surprises at the same time.

For those of you who aren't schooled musicians and don't think of music in technical terms, I suggest you think of music in terms of color. The verses should be lighter shades than the chorus. If you have a mint green verse, the chorus should be emerald. Starting with the first note of the song, the music should gradually build up to the brighter, stronger color of the chorus, using every shade and tint along the way. Pink verse, red chorus. When I listen to "Maybe It Was Memphis", I hear a soft yellow verse building into a bright red-gold chorus. I think I settled on yellow because the one time I was in Memphis on business, it was August, hot, very dry and <u>looked</u> yellow. Each of us will hear different colors. However, we all hear the same shading.

THE BRIDGE

The bridge is a musical and lyrical section that is only played once, usually after the verse and chorus have been repeated twice. The melody, lyric and rhythm of the bridge should be completely different from the verse and the chorus. Look at "I'll Make Love To You", which comes later in this chapter and see how the bridge comes in with a lot of rhythmic punch. It isn't expected and gives the song a big lift after the verses and chorus have been repeated

twice each. The bridge hasn't been heard before in the song and surprises us.
See, there's that word again. Surprise. A bridge simply connects the middle
and the end of the song by adding a major surprise to a tune we think is just
going to repeat itself.

I should tell you that I've never met a songwriter - no matter how successful
he/she is - who enjoys or feels inspired when it comes to writing bridges. One
of my very talented clients in Japan agonizes over every single bridge he writes,
and he's very prolific. I know when I talk to him each Friday afternoon, he is
hoping that just this one time, he can get away without a bridge. He always
writes one eventually, and it's usually terrific, but he never looks forward to it.
A colleague of mine who became Vice President of Music at a major studio,
sums up bridge work this way: "When I die, if, by some miracle I get into
Heaven, it will be on the condition that God wants me to rewrite the bridge".

To decide whether or not you need a bridge, time your song. If you've
repeated the verse and chorus twice and your tune comes out to be under two
minutes, add a bridge. Otherwise, just repeat the chorus and end your song that
way. A bridge can go up or down melodically in the beginning, but in power
ballads it usually goes soaring upward at the end into the last, dramatic chorus.

One of the best examples of an effective bridge is still in the old song "I
Write The Songs," which was sung by Barry Manilow. Bruce Johnston's
melody is a smooth, high soaring ballad as it comes out of the chorus. Then
when the bridge begins, the melody starts to bounce and build in the line about
music making you want to dance and getting your spirit to take a chance. Then
the emotional power keeps growing until the part about the "worldwide
symphony" takes us right back into the last chorus, which goes up a third for
greater impact.

As an ongoing exercise to strengthen your melodic skills, play your favorite
songs all the way through on your instrument and see how the musical sections
change. If you don't play an instrument, listen to the way the colors of the
music change and intensify, softening in the verses and building back up to the
chorus. Feel those changes and incorporate them into your writing style. Your
songs should have those same dramatic, unexpected jolts, too.

With so much music being created these days, and with such great access in
our work places, homes, offices, cars, dental offices and elevators, it's easy to
"borrow" someone else's melody without realizing it.   One of your
responsibilities as a composer is to be thoroughly knowledgeable about every
song on every CD. It sounds like an overwhelming task, I know, but it's your
job to be aware of what other people in your field have already done so you
don't duplicate or infringe on their work. If you were a scientist who wanted
to invent something, wouldn't you check around carefully first to be sure you
weren't duplicating someone else's effort? I know I would. I'd hate for you to
think you'd written a hit, have you make an expensive demo, get it to the
number one group that's about to release it and <u>then</u> find yourself slapped with
a major lawsuit that could wipe you out forever. Know the literature of your

craft. Be aware of everything that's gone before you. Keep current with the radio. Then, when you write a melody, you can be sure it's yours and yours alone.

Exercise

Write a melody to the lyric you just wrote to the tune of "Maybe It Was Memphis". You have a well-structured lyric to use as your guide. Put one note of music on each syllable of the lyric. Make sure as you sing the new song that you stress the words as you would when speaking them. Don't put the emphasis on the wrong syllable. You can change the rhythm of the verses to 3/4 (waltz time), 5/8, 2/2, 7/11 or whatever you like. Nothing has to be the same as it is in the original melody except the form - ABAB. You can write a bridge if you want to, but for your first few songs, it isn't mandatory. Make sure that your melody goes up into the chorus, and I recommend a jump of a major third.

If, after doing this exercise, you like the results, and you want to keep writing melodies but don't happen to have any new lyrics yet, take the words to songs you love that are on the radio and write new melodies to them. When you eventually find a collaborator, you'll have a lot of tunes ready to give him/her. Just don't tell your new partner you used a model, or he/she will be intimidated by the other set of lyrics.

Even if you are uncomfortable writing melodies to lyrics, write a couple more this way to get used to the form. Then you might try writing melodies first and creating the lyric later. But continue to start with a title, even if it's a nonsensical one like "Banana Bandana." It will help keep you focused.

Most songs on the radio are about love and probably always will be. But you can take any idea and make it into a love song. If you're obsessed about a race car, you could structure your song so that a love affair takes place near a race track. You can use car analogies in the lyric plus the power of the music to imitate the force, drive and urgency of the race - and still have a love song.

But remember - *a hit melody is a series of single notes joined together in a memorable, but unexpected pattern.* It's not a bunch of gnarly sounds or rhythm riffs you found on your synthesizer. A melody is what you sing in the shower. It's what you whistle, what you hum, what you play with one finger on the piano. One test of whether a tune will be a hit or a miss is if you can play it in seven notes or less and recognize it like they did on "Name That Tune." If you think you can fill in the holes with background vocals or slick riffs, or "fix it in the studio", you're really acknowledging the melody's weaknesses and inability to stand up on its own.

Because of the dazzling wizardry of synthesizers, it's easy for composers to fall into what I call the "technical toy trap". That's when they start to rely on their instruments or machines to do their creating for them. In order to avoid this pitfall, try to hear the melody in your head first. Don't just play or strum

MAYBE IT WAS MEMPHIS

Words and Music by
MICHAEL ANDERSON

Look-in' at you through a mis-ty moon-light, Ka-ty-did sing like a sym-pho-ny.
Read a-bout you in a Faulk-ner no-vel. Met you once in a Wil-liams play.
Ev'-ry night now since I've been back home lie a-wake, drifting in my mem-o-ry.

Porch swing sway-in' like a Ten-nes-see lul-la-by, mel-o-dy blow-ing through the wil-low tree.
Heard a-bout you in a coun-try love song, sum-mer night beau-ty took my breath a-way.
Think a-bout you on my ma-ma's front porch swing talk-ing that way so soft to me.

What was I s'posed to do? Stand-in' there look-in' at you,

To Coda ⊕

Mem- phis, _____ may - be it was South-ern _ sum-mer nights. _ May-be it was

you, _ may-be it was me, but it sure felt right. _____

chords and wait for the notes that fall in between to bounce out at you. *Hear the music in your head.* Once you write the simple melody line of the tune, then, of course, go to your instrument to embellish it. But don't rely on your instrument or synthesizer to do your initial creating for you. Rely on your gut, your heart, to tell you what you're feeling and what needs to be translated into music.

Many of my new clients who play guitar often write weak melodies. The guitar is a great rhythm instrument, but since most guitarists can't pick out individual notes, they simply play chords. I've urged thousands of songwriters to switch to a keyboard when creating their melodies, and write note by note. Then when the tune is finished, I suggest they go back to their guitars and add the chords. They are usually happily surprised with the results, which are more tuneful tunes, not just predictable chord progressions.

Many clients who don't write lyrics tell me that they only write "instrumentals" and don't want to deal with the lyrics. Some cite the success of the one, lonely instrumental per year that makes it to the charts. A few composers go so far as to tell me their melodies don't need words. But I point out to them that there is usually only one hit instrumental record every year, if that, and since absolutely every vocalist and group needs whole songs with lyrics to sing, you have the very least chance for success if you write instrumentals only. I suggest to my clients who insist their music doesn't need words, that they make a deal with their egos: for every instrumental piece they write for themselves, write one song with words and music for the marketplace. That way they allow themselves to continue doing what they love best, but they also greatly increase their chances of success by writing complete songs.

JOINT WORK

If you write lyrics only or tunes only, you should know that once a lyric is added to a pre-existing melody, it becomes a joint work. Even if that piece of music is played instrumentally thereafter, the lyricist is considered co-author, and is half owner of the copyright. I've just filed a lawsuit over "An American Hymn", the Domingo song I mentioned earlier. My composer partner is not getting enough oxygen, and feels he can still claim the tune as a separate work. This winter, Michelle Kwan, the brilliant, young ice skater, used our song as her skating music when she prepared for the Olympics, and when I called ASCAP to find out what these international performances would be worth, I was told my name wasn't even on the copyright. So make sure you get everything in writing, and never trust anybody, especially a friend. In this business, friends go south very quickly, especially when there is a lot of money at stake.

Enjoy your creative process. Writing is supposed to be fun. Don't push yourself too hard. Creating takes time. Give it to yourself. It may take a day, a week or a month. That's fine, because when something beautiful or catchy is finished, all we remember is the song, not the struggle that went into creating it. I'd rather have a half-finished tune that sparkles and promises to be special, than a dozen completed songs that are iffy at best, and sound like everything else I've already heard.

By now, you've written a brand new ABAB lyric that is well-structured. And you've written a brand new melody to that wonderful lyric of yours. Congratulations! You've just written what could be your first hit!

The more you write, the better you get. The more you write, the easier it is to write. And the more you write, the better your chances are that each new song will be your first million seller. Now let's study the structure of another smash hit.

I'LL MAKE LOVE TO YOU
(by Babyface)

Close your eyes, make a wish and blow out the candle light
For tonight is just your night
We're gonna celebrate all through the night

Pour the wine, light the fire, girl your wish is my command
I submit to your demands
I will do anything you need only ask

Chorus:
I'll make love to you like you want me to
And I'll hold you tight, baby, all through the night
I'll make love to you when you want me to
And I will not let go till you tell me to

Girl relax, let's go slow, I ain't got nowhere to go
I'm just gonna concentrate on you
Girl are you ready - it's gonna be a long night

Throw your clothes on the floor, I'm gonna take my clothes off too
I made plans to be with you
Girl whatever you ask me you know I could do

Chorus:

Bridge:

Baby tonight is your night
And I will do you right
Just make a wish on your night
Anything that you ask I will give you the love of your life...

As of this writing, "I'll Make Love To You" is number one on <u>Billboard's</u> Hot 100 pop songs, and has been for three weeks. My guess is it'll stay there for a long time, and win a truckload of awards. The song has an AABAABCB structure, a variation of AABAB: two short verses of identical melody back to back, followed by a chorus, followed by two more verses of identical melody back to back, followed by a second chorus that is the same as the first, followed by a bridge, then a final chorus.

Try to see how the lyric "looks" as you listen. Feel the rhythm and music repeat from verse one to verse two. Note the length of the lines. They are irregular and unpredictable. That's good because usually the fewer the syllables, the more creative the composer can be with the music.

There are three lines of lyric in the first A section, three more matching lines in the second A section. Then we come to the chorus, which has four lines, really two that are repeated. The second half of the song is a complete musical repeat of the first, with a four line bridge added.

While there are few original pictures in this lyric other than the clothes on the floor, the melody is gorgeous and the song is very sexy, sensuous, romantic and emotional. It sings about a scenario we all wish we could have every night - someone dedicating the evening to making us happy. So this song fulfills a fantasy, and appeals to everyone, from the little guy who sweeps the sidewalk to the president of a corporation.

One of the main purposes of a song is to give the listeners something intense and emotional that is missing from their day to day lives. A passionate love song fulfills the same fantasy that afternoon soap operas do. It offers an escape from an existence that is generally mechanical, humdrum and routine. This kind of song gives us the fantasy of love that is generous, pampering, won't hurt a bit and will guarantee a night to remember forever. Who could say no to that?

We, as the audience, become the singer, the feeling of these intense, romantic emotions. For two minutes of so, we are larger than our little lives, experience the romance and adventure of the song, feel like more and take away something to dream about. Your goal as a songwriter is to make sure your audience has something special to take away, too, when your song is over.

I'LL MAKE LOVE TO YOU

Words and Music by
BABYFACE

Exercise

Write a new lyric to the melody "I'll Make Love To You", substituting one new syllable of lyric for each syllable of lyric in the original song. Try not to add any extra ones. You don't want to tamper with a beautiful melody and wonderful rhythm. In your version, I want you to put your title in the first line of the chorus. There are five syllables in that line, which fits our guideline of seven beats or less for the title.

Now that you have a well-structured AABAABCB lyric all ready to go, write a new melody to it. Again, you might have to remove yourself from it for a few days to get the old melody out of your head.

When you get the melody finished, you'll have completed your second well-structured commercial song. That's cause for celebration! I'm very proud of you! I want you to be, too.

Your next assignment is to do something terrific for yourself as a reward for all of your hard work. This could be the most important step in the creative process. I like to buy myself flowers. Perhaps for you it's ice cream, theater tickets or a new sweater. You might want to take a drive in the country to celebrate. Whatever it is you do, make a point of acknowledging that you're doing it as a reward for what you've just created. It is a victory in itself, just because you did it - not because your song sold a million copies or was heard six times an hour on the radio. The victory starts with you.

One of my most determined clients has made great strides in her writing in just four sessions with me. But she seems to have reached a plateau, and I'm convinced it's because she can't tell herself she's done a good job. At least she's aware of the problem. And we're working on it.

This is a hurdle many songwriters have to overcome. Though they're thrilled with their writing and with the new approaches they learn, there is a part of their creative ego that is terribly frustrated and feels they should have hits immediately. Don't let past attempts and failures get in your way. The songs you wrote two or twenty years ago that missed have absolutely nothing to do with what you're doing now. As far a I'm concerned, they don't exist. It isn't fair to contaminate your new work with the unfulfilled dreams and demands of your old material.

So be fair to yourself. I don't care if you've been writing for years and haven't gotten any place yet. By the time you finish this book, you'll have a lot of valuable information you never had before - or to which you were never receptive before. You'll be a better writer just for taking the initiative to find out what you *should* be doing that you're *not* doing. That is a tremendous step.

If you reward yourself sufficiently, your creative ego will be happy to accommodate you the next time you set out to write your feelings down on paper. It will be a little easier because you've already done it and acknowledged it with something immediate and tangible. Be sure you reward yourself for everything you write - a phrase, a title, a little swatch of melody. It'll help keep your creativity flowing.

Exercise

Listen to ten songs you love. Determine whether they are ABAB songs or AABAB songs. See if any of them has a C section. Notice where the titles are placed. See if the melody of the chorus goes up. Time the songs. See how many are love songs.

When you've listened to these ten, study one new song each day for a month. Choose some from stations you don't normally listen to. In fact, one of the first assignments I give my new clients is to change all the buttons on their car radios. Make that your assignment, too. You'll thank me later. Meanwhile, you'll be learning the intrinsic value of structure in hit songwriting.

RHYMING

Great songs have to say something. They are feelings, situations and stories set to music. Rhyming makes them accessible and memorable. Children are drawn to nursery rhymes and remember them easily because the repetitive sounds and rhythms stay with them. There is a child in the personality of every adult. So adults can also be reached easiest through rhyme and repetition. You could say that the simplest songs on the radio are really adult nursery rhymes.

You may ask yourself why you should lose sleep trying to make things rhyme and say something unique when all you hear are bad lyrics and bad rhymes on the air anyway. I'll answer by saying you've chosen the wrong examples: There are many songs on the radio that *do* say something extraordinary in a passionate way and rhyme at the same time. And these are the songs that tend to become big hits, and continue to be played year after year.

What is a rhyme? A perfect one is "day," "way," "hay," "gray." An imperfect one is "day," "way*s*," "hay," "gray*ed*." While I always strive for perfect rhymes in my own work and often drive my collaborators up the wall with my meticulousness, I think my songs are better as a result. It took me a long time before I could accept a near or "bastard" rhyme in a song. Rhyming can make a good song better. But obviously it's more important to write lyrics that mean something and say something in a new, imaginative way than merely to make the words rhyme.

All good lyricists feel they should go for the perfect rhyme over the imperfect one, but that it's better to say something scintillating that doesn't rhyme than just say something ordinary that does. My guess is that if Oscar Hammerstein II came down from rock and roll heaven today and tuned into a pop station, he'd be horrified by all the sloppy rhymes. But at the same time he'd probably be intrigued with the new vocabulary writers are using, all the new ways of conveying feelings, ideas and emotions.

In the end, rhyming is up to you. I use perfect rhymes. As an artist, I shouldn't impose my values on you. Stephen Sondheim uses dazzling, perfect rhymes; Billy Joel uses near rhymes. Both write brilliant songs. Neither is right or wrong. I will only say that lyric writing is a craft and rhyming perfectly is part of that craft. On the other hand, any good lyricist will also say you have to know the rules to break them.

Take "That's What Friends Are For." There are very few rhymes in the song. It sings nicely and says something special. It is not an attempt to be particularly clever or show everybody how effective perfect rhymes can be. *It is an expression of feelings set to music.* In the areas where a rhyme is called for, the lyric rhymes perfectly, but the song's *raison d'être* is more than a collection of perfect rhyming sounds.

Now let's turn to "The Greatest Love of All." Here's a song espousing the philosophy that loving yourself is the best kind of love. If you told me five years ago you had an idea for a song on this subject I'd probably have discouraged you from writing it, saying the public is more oriented toward lyrics with simpler messages that don't require too much thought. No audience wants to have to figure out what a song is saying. The general rule is to keep it simple and accessible. In addition, listeners don't like to be preached at. "The Greatest Love of All" is so well written, however, that most of its fans didn't realize there was a message in it until they had already fallen in love with it.

It barely rhymes at all. It just doesn't seem to need to. You have to be a good writer—an awfully good writer—to pull this off. A less experienced lyricist might have forced rhymes where the *music* rhymes. But lyricist Linda Creed knew her craft and presented us with a masterful, conversational lyric without a lot of rhyming. And it "sings" beautifully. Sadly enough, Linda died the week this song went to number five on the pop charts.

Most writers make their songs rhyme at the end of the line. People expect rhymes there, but in an attempt to surprise and entertain the listener you might try moving the rhymes around. Instead of writing "I wish there were a boy for me, tall and cute as he can be," you might try "I wish there were a boy for m*e,* and he'd b*e* cute and extr*emely* tall." The "e" sound carries throughout the line and makes an internal rhyme connecting the lyric in places we don't expect. It also jogs the rhythm. Remember: Your job is to surprise the audience. Don't give them what they're expecting or they'll change stations on you.

There are some rhymes I stay away from simply because they are so predictable. When you use "double," you know "trouble" and "bubble" are nearby. However, if you precede them with an unexpected adjective, your audience will be surprised. "Sweet trouble" or "Half a double" are good examples of this.

On his *Graceland* album, Paul Simon ends one line with "night." As good a writer as Paul is, I assumed "bright" or "polite" or "light" would be the rhyming word to follow. But Paul used "Fulbright"—as in Fulbright Scholarship. I was completely dazzled and kept listening.

Mack David, my old friend and mentor, and an eight-time Academy Award nominee (as well as co-writer of forty songs that received gold records), was always pushing me to "reach": "Never settle for what is just acceptable, predictable or passable. Reach. Stretch. Fly." I pass that on to you.

To date the best multisyllabic internal rhyme I've heard is in the song "Cry Me a River," which rhymes "told me love was *too plebeian*" with "told me you were *through with me'n*." "Too plebeian" and "through with me'n" are about thirty years old and are just as delicious now as they were when they were first written. This quadruple rhyme isn't just four syllables that rhyme, but four *unique* syllables.

But, you say, most words we use in our daily vocabulary don't sing. "Garbage disposal knob" isn't particularly mellifluous. Neither is "bank vault" or "hard disk." The words that are generally considered most singable, "love," "heart," "need," "want," "miss," "long," "touch" and "hold," have been used to death. Your job as a lyricist is to find a new singing vocabulary for your songs. "Orange" doesn't rhyme with anything, but it does sing. So instead of using a near rhyme, use the "or" sound in the next line a couple of times to carry out the rhyme. "I gave him m*or*e *or*anges. He n*or*mally *or*dered *mor*e pears." This way you're able to use a word that sings, has color, is a picture, isn't used very much and which, in fact, probably has been avoided because it doesn't rhyme perfectly with anything.

I have a rhyming dictionary. I also have a thesaurus. I got both of them as bat mitzvah gifts. At the time I thought they were boring presents. I obviously wasn't thinking like a songwriter. Now I never sit down to work without both tattered volumes at my side. I may not open either during the writing of a particular lyric, but I have them there for support just in case.

Some people claim that referring to a rhyming dictionary is "cheating.'' I couldn't disagree more. What the rhyming dictionary gives is a long list of possible rhyme sounds that will either provide you with the word you need or steer you in the right direction. No matter how many hours I spend at my desk, it's usually when I'm away from my writing—taking a walk or doing my ever-popular vacuuming—that the word I *do* want pops into my head.

If you use a rhyming dictionary, be careful you're not just rhyming to rhyme. Be sure you're saying what you mean. And be sure it sounds natural—like conversation. That is where the craft of lyric writing comes in. Remember: Lyrics are dialogue for singers.

Alan Jay Lerner claimed lyric writing was a low art and ranked just above photography and just under woodworking. I violently disagree. I'd proudly hold his lyrics from *Camelot, Gigi* and *Paint Your Wagon* up to the *Mona Lisa* any day.

In the introduction to his *Lyrics,* Oscar Hammerstein tells of an instance when he saw a picture of the Statue of Liberty on the cover of the New York *Herald Tribune* Sunday magazine. The photograph was a close-up of the head of the statue. Mr. Hammerstein was amazed at the details of her hairdo. The sculptor had taken as much care with Miss Liberty's hair as with the rest of her figure, even though few people, if any, might ever see it up close. Hammerstein used that illustration to make a point. When you create a work of art, you must do it as perfectly as your ability allows. You never know when your work will be carefully scrutinized.

4

THE ALL-IMPORTANT TITLE

The title of the song is crucial to its success. Given the choice of listening to a tune called "I Want You" and another entitled "Peppermint Tires," I'd take the second. So would any music publisher. And so would most program directors—the people who determine the playlist on the radio. Collectively, they listen to thousands of songs each week. The best shot you have at hooking their interest and making them *listen* to your hard work is by using a provocative, fresh title.

The title of a song is just as important as the title of a movie or book. Titles that have appeared recently on the Hot 100 include "The Future's So Bright I Have to Wear Shades," "Rain on the Scarecrow," "Secret Separation," "My Adidas," and "Do Fries Come With That Shake." Each immediately arouses my interest. I'd go out and buy them on the strength of their titles alone.

A favorite country song that reached Number One is called "Whoever's In New England." This title is particularly good because to the best of my knowledge, no other hit country song has ever had the phrase "New England" in it. Most country songs are set in Memphis, Tallahassee, Kansas City and, God save us, New Orleans. But I've never heard a country artist sing about New England before. And the only pop song I can think of with that geographical area in the title is "Weekend in New England," a big hit written by Randy Edelman and sung by Barry Manilow. So the phrase is fresh.

Furthermore, the title suggests some hanky-panky. Since it's a country song, sung with a twang by an obvious southerner, we experience a cultural clash between the North and South. I haven't heard much of that in country tunes, either. All of this makes the song more intriguing.

Think of movie titles. You might argue that film titles have no place in this discussion. But movies are marketed just like songs. They appeal to the same instincts and emotions. You can learn a lot from scanning the movie section of your newspaper and studying the titles of current, money-making films.

Consider the movie *Police Academy*. From the title we know the movie is about police trainees. That suggests something funny to me, as it certainly did to the other two hundred million people who saw it, as well as the two screenwriters who'll never have to work again. They could have called it *A Series of Funny Episodes About a Bunch of Misfits Who Decide to Be Cops,* but they didn't. Instead they chose two words and six syllables that told us just as much, but in a concise way.

Think of best-selling books. *Iacocca*—four syllables. You know who the man is—he's president of Chrysler. The title is short and snappy. It isn't *How a Poor Italian Kid Tangled with Henry Ford and Invented the Mustang.* It's just *Iacocca*. It sizzles and it sells.

How about *On Wings of Eagles?* It sounds exciting, daring, and is very visual. Like the movie *Top Gun*. Two syllables. *Crocodile Dundee* has five. How about *Gone With the Wind?* It sounds lusty and romantic to me. If it had been called *The Demise of the Old South as We Knew It,* it probably would still be sitting under a rejection slip and "My Own True Love," its beautiful love theme song, would've been in a different movie. *Winds of War* could have been called *A Fictionalized Collection of High Powered and Occasionally Smutty Events Preceding the Outbreak of World War Two.* I'm sure Herman Wouk included all this information when he called his publisher to pitch him the book. But like every other successful writer, he needed something short and catchy to hook his publisher and all the millions of people who subsequently bought and read the tome.

Some of you will argue with me, claiming that anything with a popular writer's name on it will sell. You're correct, up to a point. But most good writers who are making a living from their writing are smart about marketing. It may not be what you want to hear, but it's true. Songs have to be accessible to the public. People need a headline before they'll commit to buying a newspaper or a magazine. The title is the headline. Give it to them.

No record company will risk its investment in a hit artist on a boring title. Their business is to sell records—not to promote esoteric art. To sell records, they need hit titles that'll make the audience respond immediately.

Some might be tempted to point out the exceptions. There were a hundred songs called "Hello" years before Lionel Richie picked up his pencil and wrote his hit song with that title. One was even written by Neil Diamond. But there are certain things Lionel Richie can get away with that you and I can't. It's a fact of life in the music business.

I like Lionel Richie and turn immediately into mush upon hearing his voice and his lovely ballads. But he didn't *start out* writing songs called "Hello." His breakthrough hit—the song that established him as a major force in the music industry—was called "Once, Twice, Three Times a Lady." No matter how you slice it, *that* is a killer title. From it we know exactly what the song is about. There isn't a woman alive who wouldn't want a man to say that about her, and no romantic man who would not want to say that about the woman in his life. Your titles should be just as evocative and provocative. If you have a strong title to begin with, the song will write itself.

Country songs often have terrific titles. I recently heard one entitled "A Squirrel Went Berserk (in the First Baptist Church)." Now that is clever and catchy. It made my day. I wouldn't recommend you write a sequel to it, but see how refreshing the language is? I don't think I've ever heard the words "squirrel" or "berserk" in a song title before. Remember, songs are ear paintings. You continually have to tell your audience something new.

Many country titles seem humorous but turn out to be magic melodrama. "She's Actin' Single, I'm Drinkin' Doubles" is about a guy whose lady is out playing around while he's consoling himself at the local bar. "Nobody in His Right Mind Would've Left Her" is an excellent example of using opposites in a title. "A Hundred Percent Chance of Rain" is a strong title and one I call a power title because the phrase is used in a different way than we'd expect—in this case, in connection with the weather forecast. The best kind of title is a phrase that is usually used in a different context but means something brand new and original in terms of love. A perfect example of such a title is "Behind Closed Doors."

I had one client who wrote lovely melodies but boring titles. As an exercise, I had him go through the brand names of all the cleaning substances under his kitchen sink and see how many song ideas he came up with. For example, "Formula 409" could be the number of the motel room in which a couple is trysting. Or it could be an area code to which a phone call—secret or otherwise—is being made. I bet you never thought of that before. Once, when the Santa Ana winds were blowing in from the desert and making my lips very dry, I bought something called Lip Therapy to keep from chapping. I realized the name of that tube of moisturizer would make a great rhythm & blues title.

Exercise

Go through the shelves under your sink, look in your medicine cabinet and search your laundry room. See how many brand names you can find that'll work as double entendres. Start with "Vanish" and "Black Flag." My guess is each of you will uncover at least eight more.

Take a title expedition. Go to a store in which you don't ever shop. Look at the brand names and see how creative you can be with them as titles. Maybe "Brooks Brothers" is a song about a girl in love with twins and can't decide which one she wants to marry.

Great titles often come from putting words together that normally don't go together. "Beautiful Sadness," one of the very special songs I wrote with Lee Holdrige, is that kind of title. You can stumble on happy accidents like that while playing the dictionary game, which is described in chapter seven. You'll be surprised how exhilarating it is to discover potential titles from unexpected sources. You'll also be surprised at how much fun you can have in the process. And remember, writing should be fun.

You can't protect a title with a copyright. Technically, that means you can use the title of someone else's old song for one of your new ones. But it's bad form. If I discover a title has already been used, I'll discard it or add some words in parentheses to differentiate it from preexisting songs with the same name.

While you can't copyright a title, I think you'd be foolish to write another song called "The Long and Winding Road" or "When Doves Cry" or "I Write The Songs." Even if a publisher likes the song, when he takes it to an artist or a producer, they'll think it's the *old* song and probably won't bother listening to it. So be smart about naming your material. You're unique both as a person and as a writer. Make sure your songs reflect that.

When I started writing, my song titles were so long they wouldn't fit on a record label. They should be short and punchy. Remember my song "In My Dreams I Was Never in Omaha?" Neither does anyone else. How about the ever-popular "Take Your Suitcase Out of My Life"? Were I writing the first song now, I'd simply call it "Omaha." I'd call the second "Suitcase." When I was a beginner, if I had written "Guilty," the tune Barbra Streisand and Barry Gibb recorded (and which Gibb co-wrote), I probably would've called it "We've Got Nothin' to Be Guilty Of." Just plain "Guilty" has much more snap and punch. Again, less is more. That's something I had to learn and something you'll know instinctively with time.

When searching for a title, one trick I often use is to take a common phrase that has "life" in it and substitute the word "love." Take the phrase, "For the life of me I couldn't think of his name." Now change that to "for the *love* of me" and you've got yourself a hit title. There's a song I recently heard called "I've Got to Learn to Love Without You." See what I mean? Any title that starts you thinking you're going to hear one thing and then presents you with something else serves a double purpose. It tricks you. The audience needs that. In fact, they demand it.

One of my earlier efforts was a song written with Steve Dorff called "You Set My Dreams to Music." Most people expected "You Set My *Words* to Music." But using the word "dreams" instead gave this song title some magic and heightened romance. And it was recorded twenty-five times in eighteen months.

Titles that rhyme internally are especially powerful. My first hit was "Silver *Wings* and Golden *Rings*." (My publisher called it "Silver Things and Onion Rings.") The title works on three levels. First, there are colors in it—silver and gold. It also contains pictures—airplane wings and wedding bands. Finally, it suggests that someone is flying away and someone else is unhappy about it. This third level—conflict—is the key to any successful drama. That tug of war makes for great songs. Think of "Separate Lives" and "Against All Odds." The more star-crossed the lovers in your songs, the better.

Don't ask me where the title "Silver Wings and Golden Rings" came from. I know I wasn't smart enough in those days to sit down at my desk and invent it. It was truly a matter of inspiration. But I quickly realized how good the title was when it passed the "Snuff Garrett test." Snuff was producing hit after hit at the time and had just had a monster record with "Gypsies, Tramps and Thieves." (How's that for a title? See all the pictures it evokes in only four words?) Snuff was famous for only listening to songs with visual titles. Give him a song called "I Miss You" and he'd leave the room. But if he liked your title, he'd dance on his desk and give you the cash to buy an American car.

Gloria Sklerov, my collaborator on this song, was a staff writer for Snuff's company at the time. She instantly sensed he'd jump at the title. And he did. He presented it to one of his female artists who, unfortunately, couldn't reach the high note, so she passed. However, someone at Snuff's publishing company sent it to Larry Butler in Nashville. Larry cut it immediately with Billie Jo Spears and I received my first ASCAP Country Music Award for it the following October.

All of that frenzied activity was initiated by the title. When a *real* song person hears a title that sizzles, all hell breaks loose. Doors that used to seem welded shut swing wide open. People in pink sunglasses start taking you to lunch in restaurants with no prices on the menus. They send you cases of wine for Christmas that you could trade for a new Porsche. Your lawyer takes your phone calls and journalists learn the correct spelling of your surname. Great titles open big doors. Of course, once you get through them, make sure your songs live up to their names.

5

COLLABORATING

When you listen to a song, it should sound like a seamless work—
whether it's written by one person or five. It should *not* sound like one
person's words set to someone else's music. It is one expression. The
two components of the song—the words and the music—should feel
fused and completely integrated. The process of getting a song to that
level requires an understanding of the collaborative process.

The lyricist's job is to translate the feelings of the music into words.
The words have to "sing." They have to flow easily and comfortably
with the melody. A good, contemporary lyric is often the equivalent of
dialogue in a conversation. Eavesdrop. Write down what people say.
The chances are good you'll be able to borrow some lines of conversation for your lyrics. I had one client who was trying to be original by
using the word "imbue" to rhyme with "you." It did follow my first
rule, which is to find vocabulary that hasn't been used to death. But it
broke the conversational rule—it didn't sound natural.

Be careful not to em*pha*size the wrong syl*lab*le in order to accommodate the music. If you find you're doing that, rewrite the lyric. Maybe
the composer can restructure his phrase so the stresses are all natural
and conversational. Be aware, however, that English is commonly spo-
ken in iambic pentameter, a metrical pattern in which there are five
stressed syllables in a line. An example of this is: "The *boy* on the *bike*
rode a*head* of the *truck* on the *street.*"

Music, on the other hand, can have any meter. If you write a lyric
with long lines of iambic pentameter, you have to give the composer

freedom to take words and phrases out here and there to make the melody and its rhythm interesting. At the same time, if you have a million-dollar title, the composer should try to accommodate it. That could simply mean placing it somewhere you didn't expect him to put it.

The bottom line in any successful collaboration is flexibility. Do what's best for the song. Don't be married to a lyric or a melody no matter how long you've walked around with it in your head or on tape before you met your partner. You *have* to accommodate one another. Bending a little here and there is far better than walking around with an armful of orphan lyrics or melodies. If you're working in a collaboration, you and your partner need each other.

I want my audience to have a new experience when they hear my lyrics. But I have to be careful about being too wordy. Nobody hums a lyric. They hum melodies. That's the part of the song that first draws in the audience. It *must* prevail. If the audience likes the feel and sound of the music, then and only then will the words be heard. That may be hard for lyricists to accept at first, but it's a reality. Of course a great melody needs a strong lyric as well, but the melody draws people in initially. The lyric keeps them there.

There are three general kinds of songwriting collaborations. In the first, you work alone writing the music and lyrics. The collaboration is between your creative ego and the critic in your head. You are alone, creating and rewriting until you think your song is finished. When it is, you may feel a rush of excitement, unable to wait to play it for somebody. At four in the morning you call a friend in Iowa and scream, "Listen to this!" You play the song. Your sleepy friend says it's a smash—and you're home.

On the other hand, your friend might say he likes the lyric but doesn't like the chorus melody. Or he might love the melody but feels the lyric isn't as strong. You might argue that the song will sound better once you record it properly in a good studio. You could get defensive and say your friend's too tired or too thick to understand it. But as a professional writer, if you get a few negative comments, put the song away for a few days, divert your attention to other things and then come back to it later with fresh eyes and ears. Distance will allow you some objectivity. You might find that what your friends have said has some validity. And you might have some new ideas of your own. Objectivity is the key here. Nobody in the heat of creation can step outside his or her song and be anything but subjective. With time, you will hopefully be able to see what your song needs to get it over the top and onto the hit list.

When you write your songs alone, you have to satisfy the creator and the critic within you. Of course, the critic is never satisfied. But we'll deal with him in chapter six.

Now suppose you're a lyricist. You've been looking for a composer/collaborator for months—even years. You have a stack of good lyrics and nobody has ever written a melody to any of them that has satisfied you. Maybe there's one lyric you've written that absolutely sizzles. Everybody says it's a hit, but you just don't have the melody yet. You've tried to write it yourself but you simply haven't got melodies in you right now.

Then along comes a composer with some pomp and dazzle who sits down at your old upright, plays like Elton John, sings like Whitney Houston, and you think you've found your other half at last. Often, though, this "discovery" can become a major disappointment. The usual reason is that lyricists get too impatient. They're frustrated seeing their lyrics on paper. They want to *hear* them. But songs aren't complete without music, and while the lyricist may hold out long and hard for the right melody, there comes a time when even the best of them throws in the towel, duped by impatience into feeling he or she has found the perfect tune.

But there is a trick to telling whether or not the melody is a hit. Listen to your collaborator's tune apart from the lyric. Ask yourself if that melody would have inspired you to write your lyric to it. If the answer is yes, you've got a match. If not, you have to go back to the composer. Be diplomatic and encouraging and tell him you feel the melody has some wonderful parts. However, you want every bar to be as good as the best ones he's already written. So you'd like him to think about an alternative to the section or sections that don't quite soar for you yet. If you approach your collaborator in a nurturing and supportive way, he or she will be encouraged to keep at it. If you sound accusing or frustrated, you could close down your partner's creativity, thereby disintegrating your collaboration.

The important thing to remember in any song collaboration is that the completed song is king. A great song is your desired goal. Your aim should be to make the song better. If you feel you're right about one section and your collaborator argues that he's right about the same section and neither of you can bully the other into submission, then the smart thing to do is for both of you to put your favorite versions aside and come up with a third one together. This is what I call finding the compromise candidate. It has worked in every successful collaboration in history and will work for you, too.

Nobody's always right. Collaborating is not a contest. Nobody should win, except the song. When it wins, everybody does. When in doubt, do what's best for the song.

If you're a composer and someone has written a lyric to one of your preexisting melodies, test that lyric by asking yourself if the lyric would have inspired you to write that melody to it. If you get a yes, fine—it's a keeper. But if you find the answer is no, be as diplomatic as possible. Suggest that this is a good beginning, and try to encourage the lyricist to dig a little deeper. Tell your partner you know he or she can come up with great lines because you've seen them in other work. Anyone who's done it once, can do it again. You're expecting great things. That's why you wanted to work with this writer in the first place. It's all positive reinforcement.

Above all else, be diplomatic. Often a careless, offhand remark can so undermine a writer's confidence that he or she is afraid to write anymore. It's a good idea to understand your partner's sensitivities and creative process. It's necessary to be as understanding of your partner as you'd like your partner to be of you.

Sometimes your collaborator will need pampering. Occasionally you might have to tell your partner something is great when it isn't just to keep him or her creating. Later, when he or she is feeling more confident, you can say you've been thinking about the song you wrote last week, wondering if there isn't a better way you can both approach the chorus. . . .

A major stumbling block for collaborators is possessiveness. Sometimes teams work exclusively with one another. They make commitments just as they do in marriages. But some collaborations are more casual, and both partners work with other people. My advice is not to focus on what you *don't* do together, but on what you *do* accomplish together.

If your partner is suddenly successful with another writer, it is natural for you to be jealous. Your partner, however, is also the co-author of many of the things you wrote, and his success is contagious. So be happy for him, acknowledge his victory, be gracious about it, and use it to give the songs you do write together a boost.

Nobody can explain why one collaboration works and another fizzles. I try to give each new association a fair shot. It doesn't always take in the first song, so try three tunes together. You'll know by then. It's either magic or it's mediocre. Period. If an old partner of yours is suddenly successful with someone else, figure your turn with your current hit-writing partner is coming up, too, and keep working.

Sometimes collaborations are a matter of convenience. You may be the only two musical people in your zip code. At first you were both in the same place in terms of your career—you had everything ahead of you and nothing but enthusiasm for your team effort. But suppose you find that your partner isn't holding up his or her end of the bargain. Maybe your collaborator is not as committed as you are to being a hit songwriter anymore. Maybe your partner is writing the same melody sideways every time you get together. Or suppose you've just outgrown your partner professionally. Maybe your melodies have been steadily improving but his lyrics aren't. What a difficult dilemma to be in! Suppose you've pushed and encouraged your partner to dig deeper and come up with something more original. And suppose it still isn't coming.

This is the time when you have to suggest you both try working with other people. Don't sever the relationship permanently, because your present partner could just be going through a slump. Something could happen in his or her life in six days or six months to trigger that spark of greatness. But you owe it to your songs to make them as good as they can be. Tell your partner you want to work with some different collaborators to try to stretch new muscles in your creative life. Put the onus on yourself—not your partner. You know in your heart when your collaboration is working. When it isn't, you have the choice of either being victim to it or taking charge of it. The people with hit songs take charge.

This breaking up process can be very tricky, especially if you write with either your spouse, your roommate or a relative. If you think working with different collaborators will damage your personal relationship and if you feel that is more important than your songwriting career, fine. Stay where you are. But if your career is important to you, you have to muster the courage to be honest. If your mate is really rooting for you, he or she will understand and wish you well. It shouldn't have any effect on your personal relationship. I always feel I can bring more to a partner when I'm the most fulfilled and satisfied from other sources. Then I bring that fulfillment to the collaboration. It makes our time together even more satisfying. And it also gives me an identity away from the relationship which is vital to me, allowing me to make a unique contribution to that partnership.

If you choose to stay with a partner you know is holding you back, eventually your resentment will contaminate the collaboration. I could make a long list of clients who were very creative but unsuccessful before they came to me. They were squashed from living or working with the wrong person. Later, when they ended their negative relationships, these same "squashed" songwriters blossomed into miraculously successful hit writers with other partners.

You may not realize it, but writing is a risk. Moving on is a risk, too. But without taking chances, we'd all live boring, safe, predictable lives. Songs can't be boring, safe or predictable. They should be inventive, exciting and right on the edge. Being a creative person involves taking risks every day of your life. Be aware of it, and make your decisions accordingly.

WORKING WITH A COMPOSER

When I write without a melody as a guide, I have too much freedom. I may write something that is articulate but dull from a rhythmic point of view. I tend to use too many syllables. While I know better, there is a part of me that wants to paint a more vivid picture in the lyric or describe an emotion in greater detail. Then I end up with long lines of fifteen or sixteen syllables each and wonder why my collaborator can't come up with a melody that sizzles. So for me, being in the room with the composer and writing simultaneously works best. That way I don't go off on any tangents and my partner doesn't have to go through my lyric eliminating all my hard-sought adjectives.

Obviously this process works best when I'm collaborating with someone I trust. That means I can suggest a terrible line or phrase and not worry that my partner is going to think I can't do any better. I may come up with forty turkeys, but my partner knows from past experience that idea forty-one could be the gem we've been waiting for all day.

Trust is the major ingredient in any successful collaboration, because you give each other permission to risk being bad. You know how to deal with the near-misses. You've learned from your past experiences together how to urge your partner on in a new direction when he or she has been stumbling with the same stuck melody or lyric all day. Trust. Without it, you are auditioning, not writing. You should write from strength, not fear. That is just as true when you write and compose by yourself.

Whichever method of collaboration works best for you, it's vital for you to understand the subtleties of the relationship. Then if something isn't working, you can stand back and be objective. Ask yourself: "If my friend was having this problem, what would I suggest my friend do?" Take your own advice. In a successful collaboration you shouldn't try to dominate or control another person. Your job is to write hit songs.

The songs are what count. You have to do what is best for those songs. Ultimately, what's best for them will be best for you, too.

When I collaborate, I try to set the appointment for the time when I am most creative. In my case, it's first thing in the morning. While I could jump out of bed and immediately address Congress, I find out what my partner's best time is and try to compromise on what's good for both of us. If he or she is a night person and wakes up at four in the afternoon, that signals trouble. But as professionals interested in doing what's best for our songs, we try to find a balance. Then I do creative exercises to get ready, so that when I walk into my partner's office, I'm set to work and don't have to waste an hour revving up.

The most successful teams are made up of people who have respect for each other's craft and for each other's time. You are equals. Remember that. On the first few occasions in my life when I worked with "stars," I felt so insecure I wrote badly. But now I write feeling like a star myself. I'm pumped up and ready for anything. And on my best days, I write like a champion. If you feel insecure, your partner will feel the same way. Then instead of ending the session with a hit, you write a disaster. If necessary, trick yourself into feeling confident. Keep repeating "I'm a terrific songwriter, I have something unique to say and this collaboration is working!" Pretty soon you *do* feel confident and your partner picks that up and you're on your way.

Tell your partner what you expect from him beforehand. It's not fair to be suddenly furious with him for lapsing into yoga on the piano top if he didn't know you find such behavior unacceptable. Too many songwriters seem to be on day passes from the Home for the Nearly Normal as it is. Each person has different expectations. It's always best to check out your collaborator's quirks in advance. Do your homework. Make the collaborative experience as comfortable as possible.

Collaborations should be overhauled every few months just like cars. If you haven't evaluated your musical relationships lately, here are some questions to help you do that:

Collaborator's Check List

1. Are you happy with your collaborator? If so, why?
2. Are there areas in your work together that need improving? What are they?
3. What do you think you can do to improve your working relationship?

4. What do you want your collaborator to do to improve your working relationship?
5. How long have you worked together?
6. What success have you had as a team?
7. Do you think it's impossible for you to reach this level of success or beyond with anyone else?
8. Does the thought of a change scare you?
9. Do you see yourselves as partners in ten years?
10. How do you get over your crises as a team?
11. Is there someone else you'd prefer to work with instead of your partner?
12. Is there someone you'd want to work with in addition to your present partner?
13. Are your songs as good as they can be? If not, why?
14. What can you do about it?
15. What do you like best about what you bring to the collaboration? List ten things.
16. What do you like best about your partner? List ten things.
17. List all the valuable contributions you bring to the collaboration.
18. List twenty-five reasons why your partner should be happy writing songs with you.
19. List all the ways you can improve your writing relationship together.

MAKING TIME TO WRITE

6

I know what it's like to have great ideas surging through you but no time to write them down. Most songwriters have other jobs. Those jobs are usually time-consuming and draining. Then when you get home you have families and bills and landlords and laundry to deal with, so when do you get time for yourself? How do you make room for your songs?

To me, songs are like children. If your child was in need of your time, wouldn't you give it to him? So give your songs the same consideration. Whenever you're torn, keep thinking of your song as something you created that brings you pleasure but needs some of your quality attention. You know it will give back to you everything you give and more.

We're all plagued with voices telling us we're not writing. Even when we *are* writing, the voices tell us we could be doing more and doing better. That is the critic at work. Usually writers wrestle with this critic until they understand his dynamic and develop a system of controlling him.

When I finish a writing session, I tell myself out loud that I did a good job, that a few great lines are a terrific start and I should be very proud of myself. This kind of affirmation helps to drown out the critic who will never give you credit for doing anything right. You have to learn to recognize this guy. He's seductive. First he'll tell you that you've *got* to work today. He nags you until you can't procrastinate any further. Even when you get down to your song he judges the value of what you've put on paper—all negatively. When you finish your daily assignment, you probably are thrilled and full of joy and pride. But this guy goes right into high gear and challenges you: "Okay, so you've got a song. But who in the world's going to sing it? Who ever heard of you? How are you going to get this to an artist who means something? Maybe you should just throw it out with the garbage."

Obviously this critical voice is destructive. What you have to do as a professional writer is acknowledge its presence but remember that you have two ears. Remember that in the other ear, you have the creative, purely inspired voice telling you that what you've done has a great hook, is exquisite, powerful, emotional, lasting and meaningful. And as you do with a stereo system, you can learn to adjust the volume of the critic's voice so your own supportive voice broadcasts louder.

Writers who don't have time to write envy writers who do. But let me share a secret with you. Writers who have all day to write welcome distractions so they don't *have* to work. I've found that what works best for me is to schedule an appointment with myself to write, just as I would schedule an appointment with a publisher, a beautician or a masseur. I can't change or cancel the appointment. I set aside time from my day for the writing process. I mark it in my appointment book—in ink. I only write during those hours or minutes. I don't take phone calls or answer the door while I'm working. I don't allow any interruptions. Once I make the commitment to spend this time writing, I honor it. It'll work for you, too.

I'm most creative early in the morning. If I weren't a writer I'd make a great newspaper boy. I find if I get out of bed and go directly to work, I can put in a couple of good hours before the phone starts ringing— before people and other responsibilities start invading my day.

But I'm a morning person. Some of you are comatose until noon. And then you're at work doing your day job. How do you concentrate there? And when you get home from work, the baby's crying and the older kids are throwing mud at your wife? You'd kill for a hot shower but the power has been turned off because you spent too much for your last demo and the Con Edison people don't consider your music a priority? Where in the midst of this chaos are you going to find time and space to write love songs?

First, create a place for yourself where you can shut out all distractions. Maybe it's the basement. Perhaps it's the garage. Or maybe it's the back seat of your car in the garage. I have one client who sits on the floor of her closet with her terrific, inexpensive portable Casio keyboard and headphones. While it's probably more practical to have a separate room in which to work, those of you who don't might look into the closet approach. It certainly is private.

Set down rules. You are not to be disturbed, except in case of fire. Even then, if it's only the kitchen that's in flames and you're in the bedroom, leave word with the firemen not to noodge you unnecessarily until you complete your time commitment to yourself.

If finding peace in your house is impossible, go to a park or a coffee shop. Take your portable keyboard and guitar and your notebook, and plan to spend twenty minutes there, deliciously alone. Nobody doesn't have twenty minutes. You may not have two hours, but you *do* have twenty minutes. With just that short span of time ahead of you, you'll be excited to take advantage of it. You'll be amazed how productive you can be. No matter how successful we become, it's still better to wish we had more time to write than wish we had more to write about.

As important as it is to make time to write, it's also essential for any successful writer and artist to know when he or she needs a day off. My friend Carol Sobieski is one of the busiest and best screenwriters in the world. She's in great demand and is *always* working. But once every ten days or so she takes a day off, gets a roll of quarters and a large box of Tide and heads out on a laundry run to visit her three children who are all in boarding schools. This recreational time is very valuable to Sobieski (she prefers to be called by her surname), since she always comes back filled with stories of the road and experiences of her kids that exasperate but at the same time nourish and enrich her.

Focus and commitment are essential to your success, but so is time away from your work once in a while. You need new experiences to write about and keep you balanced.

A writing teacher of mine said he liked to take his notebook to museums, where he would park on a bench and work in the crowded halls. He claimed the more noise he had to drown out, the deeper he would have to concentrate. He came up with ideas he wouldn't have gotten if he had just stayed home and didn't have to focus so sharply.

One of my clients, who is from a farm in Texas but now lives in a tiny, crowded apartment in Long Beach, can't work at home. He needs more space to feel comfortable writing. What he does is take his guitar and drive to the parking lot of the Queen Mary and write for two hours in his car. He also follows every writing session—no matter how productive—with a chocolate espresso in the Queen Mary coffee shop. Whatever works, do it.

I've noticed that when I have the least time to write but have set aside at least a few minutes to *try* to write something, I get the most done. When I remove the *demand* from the task, the part of my creative ego that has been squashed with "shoulds" can flourish. You wouldn't expect to come up with a killer title or a great hook with just eleven minutes left before an important meeting on some other project, would you? But that's when I do my best work. When I'm seeing clients and have only a small part of each day to work on my own songs, I write infinitely better than when I have the whole day ahead of me just to write. One good, productive hour is much more valuable to me than a whole day of mediocrity. Like many writers, I suffer greatly from isolation. While I resist it, I can spend six or eight hours alone at my piano or desk if I know I'll be seeing somebody after I finish work. Consequently, I schedule a lot of dinner dates. It works well for me. You can try it, too.

Let's go back to your park or coffee shop. Say you put in your twenty minutes. Now you have to be back at work. Chances are you've got something new on the pages of your notebook. You may not think it's what you were after initially, but you have something. Be sure to check off in your appointment book that you kept the meeting with yourself to write that day. This way you acknowledge you met the commitment. You know you've spent twenty minutes writing and you have words and notes on a page to prove the time was productive. You reluctantly head back to your job, wishing you could just stay put for another half an hour and get the song finished.

Your reluctance to end your songwriting session is normal. But you'll have something to start with the next time you schedule an appointment with yourself. Besides, while you may think you've stopped writing, your subconscious knows that's false. It never stops. It's like one of those twenty-four-hour 800 numbers. There's always someone on duty.

I think of my mind as being much like a computer bank. It has information stored away on files that may be hard to retrieve. But if I send in a request for information (notice I didn't say "demand"), the little microchips in my brain take the request and then seek out the file containing that particular information. While I think I'm just driving my godson to the baseball-card store or picking up clothes at the dry cleaners, my subconscious is on red alert, seeking out the new ideas for which I left a request earlier in the day or week. And when I'm watering my plants or baking, an idea will suddenly come to me. Of course I write it down. And if I haven't the time to address it right then and there, at least I have something to start with for my next writing appointment.

I work best when I write every day. Even if it's just twenty minutes at a time, I try to write something on a daily basis. That way I'm always ready to write. I don't have to spend my precious writing time warming up the way I would if I had missed a day or a week in between writing sessions.

I don't always write songs. Sometimes I'll write a little letter to myelf reminding me how well I did the day before. Sometimes I'll write a note to the gardener begging him to save my gardenia bushes. I might rewrite that letter nine times. But the point is, no matter what I'm putting on paper, it's all *writing*.

No matter what is on the page, I always try to enjoy the writing process. I constantly make it fun for myself. If I feel stuck on a serious, intense love song based on a true life adventure, I'll scribble four lines all rhyming with "zickle," which is a silly-sounding word and one I've never used in a song, just as an exercise to warm up.

I recently returned from a marvelous trip to Martha's Vineyard and had to write a thank-you note to my host and hostess. I was so exhausted and jet-lagged my first day back I couldn't compose even a brief letter that didn't sound hideously boring. What made it worse was knowing that my host was a sensational writer. Both he and his wife are world-class wits, and I knew they were expecting something other than "Thanks for the hospitality. Love, Molly." So instead of a traditional, socially acceptable thank-you note, I wrote them a thank-you limerick. I had fun with it. I fulfilled my social commitment. I used words I'd never been able to use before in songs. I felt accomplished. And with the rush and satisfaction from that brief five-minute exercise, I was then ready to work on a love song.

I prefer to write for two or three hours every day, but during my busiest periods, when I'm lecturing across the country, I find my writing time gets whittled away until I'm left with only Sundays for uninterrupted writing. This used to be catastrophic. It ranked right up there with the plague and having to go to traffic school—again. But now I've learned to trust myself to use that time wisely and well. I know from past experience that when I just have a few hours, I perform brilliantly. That gives me the courage and incentive to take what I *do* have, pull out all the stops and go for it.

With all the lectures and seminars I give, I find myself spending more and more time on planes. For some reason I'm always on the toddler flights. I honestly think the airlines gather up children—the cuter the better—and arrange for them all to be crying at the same time so I can't concentrate.

I was a baby once myself. But I can't walk up and down the aisles singing "Mary Had a Little Lamb" all the way to Omaha. So what I do is lock myself in the bathroom. I know it may sound selfish, but with four or five hours during which no ringing telephone can disturb my writing process, I intend to make the best of my time in the air. Even if there weren't babies crying on the planes, there are always flight attendants conspiring to ply me with Pepsi, little square chickenettes and reconstituted pea pods. Being in a tourist-class seat is no place to write. Not for me anyway.

I've done well in the lavatories of the friendly skies. There is no place I've ever been that is more uncomfortable or more crowded. There is absolutely nothing else I can do in there to distract myself. So when I enter with my notebook, I come out with songs. The flight attendants are often concerned about me, but on leaving I smile and assure them it was just a touch of the *touristas.*

Please note that with the exception of my recent trip to Martha's Vineyard on a nine-passenger Cessna (there was no bathroom on that aircraft—they replaced it with a chapel), I only fly on large planes. So there's always more than one bathroom. I'm not recommending airplane lavatories to everyone—it just happens to work for me.

For those unscheduled bursts of inspiration, always keep a pad and pencil next to the phone, in your pocket, purse and car. You never know when you'll be stuck in traffic for ten minutes. Instead of leaning on the horn like your fellow drivers, you can be working on a hit song.

Always keep a writing pad and pen next to your bed. Our subconscious minds are the most free just before we drift off to sleep. Don't let a good idea get away because you're too tired to go get your writing pad. Never trust yourself to remember it in the morning. You *won't.*

You should also have a separate notebook just for titles and ideas. That way, when you're feeling a little dry, you just have to open your book and the ideas you gathered on more inspired days are right there waiting for you to develop them.

Please do me one major favor. Promise me that all of your notebooks will be ring-bound so your precious pages can't be torn off or fly away. I never trust my ideas to yellow legal pads. (Lawyers might, but I don't trust them either.) It's too easy for loose-leaf pages to get lost. Ideas are the only resources I have. So each time a notebook is full, I put the date on the cover, just like I do on my checkbook, and file it. That way I have every draft of every song I ever wrote. If anyone ever wants a rewrite (and they always do—even if the song's already been a hit), I have all of my alternative drafts right there.

I believe ideas fly through the air into our minds. If we don't think enough of these ideas to commit them to paper, they'll get insulted and fly out of our heads into someone else's. So cherish your inspirations and be sure to keep careful track of them all.

However many days per week you write, be sure your appointment book reflects that total at the end of the week. Add up the hours. Keep a running tally. There's a tremendous sense of accomplishment in knowing you put in the time and kept your commitments. You will also come to realize that with all that quality time spent in writing, great results are imminent.

You should reward yourself after each writing session—even if the session only lasts twenty minutes. The creative part of our personalities is a child. And the child needs a reward. Give it to him. Then next time you want to trot him out to work, he'll remember you took good care of him, bought him a surprise and made it fun afterward. So he'll be more willing to work with you next time if you take good care of him now.

Writing a little every day is like oiling machinery to keep it functioning at a high level of efficiency. I was advised to run the air conditioner in my car for a few minutes once a week even during the winter to make sure the system will work when I need it on hot, muggy summer days. I pass the same suggestion on to you about your writing. I know it works.

For those of you who have time to write but don't use it for writing, it could very well be you just don't *want* to write at present. Maybe you should spend the time reading or gathering new experiences to write about in the future. The creative process cannot be compared to working on an assembly line. There, you have to show up for work each day and put together a required number of widgets within an eight-hour period. But as a songwriter, you will have days that are seemingly productive and others that aren't. On the ones that aren't, give that time to yourself anyway. If you've set aside an hour to write and have a blank page when it's up, at least write, "I kept my appointment with myself today. I'm very proud of myself. I've finished writing for today and my subconscious will take over from here. It has never let me down. I expect surprises in the wind."

There's a few lines right there, see? And it's all nurturing. Nothing is harder on a writer than that awful, persistent, nagging critic's voice saying you're not doing it correctly or you're wasting your life, throwing away money and time you could spend more wisely on other things. Shut that voice up. He's a bad guy.

In the case of one client, the voice was so loud I told him to give it a tangible form and put that object in a drawer while he wrote. He decided it was an ugly old dirty ashtray. He put it in his upper-right-hand desk drawer while he wrote. When he was finished, he took it out again and showed the ashtray he had written something wonderful. Trembling at first, he steadily gained momentum and control until he finally overpowered the bad guy. Now he doesn't listen to his critic much anymore. With practice, you'll be able to overpower yours, too, and the time you make to write will be well spent creating hit songs.

At the end of each writing session, answer these questions:

1. Did you get a good idea today?
2. Did you write it down in your permanent notebook?
3. Did you make and keep an appointment with yourself to write today?
4. Was it a productive session? List everything you accomplished: verse, chorus, bridge, title.
5. When is your next appointment with yourself?
6. What have you done to reward yourself for honoring your time commitment and your good work? List three things.

7

STIMULATING CREATIVITY

Some of us are lucky. We have so many sparkling, exciting, fresh ideas, we'll never run out. But others may find from time to time in their creative lives that they're going a little dry. If you find you've been writing the same thing sideways in your last several songs and your melodies are all starting to sound alike, it's natural to feel nervous and a little frightened for your creativity. You swear you're doomed to spend the rest of your life wistfully remembering the exhilarating days of fire and thunder when you were getting great ideas and writing hits.

But you *can* do something about it. You don't have to play victim to your muse. You can be inspired by another one. Here are some exercises that my successful clients and I have done when we're feeling dull, sluggish and unable to squeeze anything memorable from the air.

First, you should recognize that the creative process is cyclical. While your subconscious never stops working, your conscious mind *does* need a day off now and then. Use this time to gather new experiences instead of staying home, groaning and beating yourself up.

Get out of your house or office or wherever it is you usually write. Close the door to that area, both figuratively and literally. Head for a place you've never been. I usually go to the same restaurant for breakfast every day. But when I'm stuck and feeling stale, I change my pattern. Instead of wearing my comfortable old sweatsuit and meeting people I already know, I put on eyeliner and my best new clothes and go someplace where I don't know anyone. In a foreign environment I see new things. I feel new things, hear new things, smell new things.

Instead of having my usual peppermint tea, I might have a café au lait or espresso. My taste buds are treated to new experiences.

Eavesdrop. If people are talking about the stock market, don't ignore them, thinking your songs are about love, not economics. Listen to what's being said even if you're way over your MasterCharge limit and your checks are bouncing. If nothing else, you'll learn something, hear some vocabulary you normally don't use or think to use in love songs. Your brain will store these words and phrases. I believe that for every new idea our brains receive, a little red neon sign flashes in the gray cells that says "interesting, stimulating, give me more." And the devoted librarians at the conservatories of music in our minds file it all away in the appropriate departments.

Strike up a conversation with a stranger. Make up a new identity. Tell your breakfast partner you're a pediatrician or a test pilot or the social secretary for the governor's wife. Become that person for twenty minutes. Don't worry if you blow it. This is a game. It's supposed to be fun. But whatever you do, don't sit there and pour out your heart to a stranger about how stuck you are. The point of this exercise is to give yourself some time off from your problem, not to compound it.

Go to a museum. Force yourself to look at works of art you might have avoided during earlier visits. You might not like Byzantine art, but check it out anyway. Not long ago I was feeling as creative as a soggy mop. I went to see the French Impressionist exhibit from the Hermitage and Pushkin museums in Russia. Not only was I totally delighted by the art, which is from my absolutely favorite period, but also I stumbled onto a Lalique exhibit I didn't even know existed. I left, my mind dancing with ideas, raced home and worked until midnight when my back quit.

So if your brain has been running on empty, realize it needs input. Give it what it wants. You don't know how it'll assimilate that information or use it later on. As a sensitive writer, you're like a vacuum cleaner. Your job is to absorb new experiences so you feel alive, enthusiastic, excited, interested and stimulated.

Go into a store you've never been in. Look at merchandise you'd never consider buying, which might be aluminum siding or the Hope diamond. Listen to the salespeople talk. They're funny. They don't need to know you're there with a secret motive. You may not need a new Ferrari just yet. Go into the showroom anyway. Act as if you're a serious buyer. Observe everything, including the other customers. Check out the sales pitch. See about financing. See if they'll take cash. Check their responses. This is your persona. You can handle it any way you want.

A successful stimulant that works for me is going to a different supermarket. At my regular market, I know where everything is. In fact, I could probably go through the place blindfolded and still find the peppermints and pâté. But when I go to a different market, I don't know where anything is. I might get mad and be tempted to walk out. But the discomfort of being in a strange environment is actually very stimulating. Once, I was in an unfamiliar market and was fuming because the checkout person was on 33⅓ rpms and I was on 78. But while I waited, I saw a guy with a walkie-talkie and a calculator. His children had a food list, as well as walkie-talkies, and they were calling in prices from other aisles. He'd enter that price on his calculator to see if they could afford that item in their weekly food budget. And they were talking like truckers—using all that "ten-four" jargon.

I loved it. I didn't care that it took forty-five minutes to purchase one pint of low-fat milk. The experience was worth it. It gave me tons of ideas. While I haven't actually used a man with a walkie-talkie and a calculator in a supermarket in any of my work just yet, that's okay. I was distracted, amused and entertained. The experience was rich and will always be with me.

CHANGE THE MENU

Speaking of supermarkets, I think we all tend to buy the same food items from week to week. So buy a couple of new items—things you've never tried. If that's too big a step, let me suggest you simply try a new brand. I know the tendency is to go with the familiar and the comfortable. But this exercise is meant to jostle you up a little, to take some risks and to have some new experiences as a result.

We do have our principles. No matter how stuck I am, I'd never buy anything other than Heinz ketchup in the squeeze bottle. Period. But I'm willing to bend in the fruit juice section. Why just a while ago I bought Minute Maid apple juice—at a substantial saving, I might add—instead of my usual Motts. It felt weird. I wondered if my metabolism would change from the new taste and I'd suddenly become tall and willowy. But see, here I was thinking about that instead of my poor, doomed song. So the exercise worked.

THE DICTIONARY GAME

It's important to have a little routine to do at the beginning of every day to make you feel that you have lots to say and an unlimited source on which to draw. I suggest you try the dictionary game. It was recommended to me by poet Charles John Quarto and it has never let me down. The game only takes a few minutes and can be a lot of fun as well as very enlightening.

To play this game, open your dictionary at random. Drop your finger down on the page. Choose the closest *picture* or *proper noun* to your fingertip. Write it on a piece of paper under the column heading "Nouns." Make sure the noun is not one you use regularly in your songs. If you land on "love" or "loneliness" or "heart," keep your finger moving down the page until you find a more unusual word.

Find nine more pictures or proper nouns in the same fashion. Make sure you don't get them all from the same letter in the dictionary. This an equal-opportunity exercise. Stop when you get ten nouns. Then do the exercise ten more times choosing adjectives you've never used in a song but would say to someone in conversation. Write the adjectves down in a column next to the nouns. Match each adjective with each noun.

Write the results on another piece of paper. Then cross-pollinate each noun with each adjective. Somewhere in this list of pairs you will stumble over something you've never thought about before. You could find a terrific title. You could find a great phrase. You could assimilate the beginning of a song. The rhythm of the words might suggest a melody.

If you get things that don't make sense, like "reindeer detergent," or "polyester pie," don't throw them away. You might want to try writing a silly song, maybe even a commercial for a fictional product. You use the same creative muscles to create a silly song as you do in writing a love song. You just have unusual subject matter. If it's fun and seemingly stress-free, you won't make the same demands on your writing that you associate with "real" songs and it'll whiz by, making you feel you're on a hot streak.

I give this assignment to each of my new clients and they have fun with it. Remember, writing is supposed to be fun. As the second part of this assignment, take one of the pairs of words from your lists twice a week and write a stream of consciousness story about each of them. Write down whatever comes into your head. Never mind spelling, punctuation, grammar or logic. It can be as whimsical or romantic as you let it be. I recommend you introduce the element of magic and the unexpected in your story. One of my clients recently found the phrase "crackerjack Porsche" by playing the dictionary game and it sparked a story about a shiny red Porsche that ran on Cracker Jacks, not gas, and so instead of zooming down the street the way those cars normally do, this Porsche bounced like popping corn. Another client found "sizzling redhead,'' but instead of writing just another story about a hot-looking woman who seduced him in a bar, he wrote a saga about a guy who was a frustrated melody writer who couldn't give away his songs on earth. He was taken by this sizzling redhead to a planet where they didn't have any songwriters—just programmers who designed rhythm tracks, and nobody had anything to sing. On this planet, everything he wrote was a hit. But then, bored with easy success, he hitchhiked home to earth. It was a marvelously creative experience for my client, who'd been feeling stale lyrically up to then, and it opened up a hot creative streak for him that hasn't stopped yet.

If you play the dictionary game every day before you start work, you'll find yourself with exciting new things to think about all the time. And with new things to think about, you'll certainly have unlimited material to write about. That way the blank page won't be your enemy, but your ally in helping you to get this endless flow of ideas committed to paper.

YELLOW PAGES

Something I do when I'm feeling a little stale is flip open the Yellow Pages, and wherever my finger drops, I call the number to ask about the services that company offers. I've learned about beekeeping, coin collecting, skylight installation and all-night dentistry. Gathering this information has the same effect as playing the dictionary game. It makes me think about new things, it's terrifically stimulating, makes me feel like I've had a little adventure and just takes a few minutes.

REROUTING

For a quick exercise out of the house, next time you're headed somewhere, take a new route. You'll see things on streets you've never seen before. Next time your car is in the shop, instead of bemoaning your lack of wheels for the day, take a bus. In Los Angeles that comes under the heading of science fiction. We usually just rent another car. But taking the bus puts you in touch with a whole new realm of experiences. You'll come in contact with people you wouldn't ordinarily meet. Observe them. How do they dress? What do they say? What are they carrying? Do they wear hats? Did they have bus passes? Did they know the driver? Did they speak English? Check everyone's shoes. What shape are they in? How many people are wearing sneakers?

Once I had to borrow my neighbor's van. Driving it after my Rabbit convertible was astounding. Riding up that high made me feel like a trucker. I assumed a different persona. I was Molly-Belle, the singing teamster, on my way to Chattanooga with a load of chickens. I drove like a maniac. It was an adventure. When it was over I was glad to have my little Rabbit back, but I was invigorated from the experience.

As creative people, we are both drawn to and afraid of new things. If we can learn to overcome the fear, we can jump into new experiences. With our curiosity about the world unleashed, we'll never be stuck for new ideas.

PHYSICAL EXERCISE

Since writing is cerebral, doing something physical works wonders for stimulating creativity. Some people jog every morning. While they're jogging and sweating like mad, their whole bodies are stimulated and invigorated. When they're exercising, these people focus on different objectives—completing that two miles or five miles or even just making it to the corner. The point is, they have short-term goals that are physically demanding but have nothing to do with writing.

If you do your five miles, you usually feel a sense of completion and pride and can then move on to the next task at hand—writing. Accomplishing something physical the first thing in your day is a wonderful way of warming up for cerebral exercise. Completing one thing gives you courage and incentive to start another.

I don't jog—I walk. I'm not lazy. I have a delicate lower lumbar region. But I still do my hour of exercise every day. I used to have a set path along which I walked every morning. Now I find deviating from that path is a lot more stimulating. Lately I was really drawn to the ocean and marked out a four-mile path along it. Currently you'll find me at sunup walking through the alleys of Santa Monica, because this week I'm having rural longings. Being unable to take a vacation just now, I trick myself into thinking I'm in the country by taking the alley route, which looks just like back roads. When I come home from my walk, I'm invigorated both physically and mentally, I take my shower and I'm all ready to write.

Though I tell myself I walk for my health, the truth is it gets me out into the world where things are going on. I can't imagine stumbling over much of interest in my kitchen, unless I've been trying to cook again and something explodes. I have to go out into the world, rather than expect the world to come to me. While I'm walking, admiring the flowers and the birds and wondering about the psychological differences between those of my neighbors who build fences and those who don't, my subconscious is at work, too, clearing out the cobwebs and getting ready for a good day at the piano or the word processor.

MEDITATION

While I may wake up ready to write in the morning, I reach a lull about midday. In order to get myself over that hump, I take the phone off the hook and meditate for fifteen minutes. During that time, I try to stop all the thoughts that have been rushing through my head like race cars on a complicated freeway system and envision only white space. I am not doing this to "get" anything, merely to give my mind a rest. I make the same commitment to meditating that I do to the rest of my work, and nothing can interrupt me.

When I first started to meditate, it was difficult making the time and sitting still that long. But like anything else, the more you do it, the easier it gets. Now I look forward to the peace and tranquility of those fifteen minutes as much as I look forward to my oatmeal in the morning. I find I'm overtaxed and cranky if I don't meditate. And I always feel refreshed and re-stimulated afterward. This is a keeper. I recommend it highly.

The wonderful thing about the brain is, the more you know, the more you want to know. It's not like a closet that gets full and closes down. A successful man once told me, When you want something done, ask someone busy to do it. That's because there's an energy, a rush that goes with activity. Somebody whose machinery is already oiled and pumping is ready to go to work. So if you're revved up with interest about the yen/dollar ratio, it is contagious and helps you with your love songs, too.

The bottom line is this: try new things, go new places, talk to new people, try new foods, drive new cars, drive down new streets, and constantly change your life patterns to allow for new experiences, which will continually surprise you. You will have new things to think about and write about with renewed enthusiasm, energy, excitement and vigor.

When you're feeling uncreative, dull and listless, here's a checklist you can use to help get back on track.

1. Did you do any exercise today? Meditation?
2. Did you play the dictionary game or the Yellow Pages game?
3. Did you take a bus or other form of public transportation?

4. Did you drive down a different street or shop at a different market? Go to a new restaurant and try something unusual?
5. Did you create a new, temporary persona and have him/her talk to a stranger?
6. Did you go to a museum?
7. Did you write a nonsense song or limerick?
8. Did you peruse a newspaper or magazine you normally don't read?

If you get all no's, choose a couple of items from the list above and do them. If you get all yes's and you're still stuck, I think you definitely need to fall in love. Nothing will give you more inspiration. If you're still stuck after falling in love, break up. That'll do it.

8

OVERCOMING WRITING BLOCKS

No writer, no matter how famous, prolific, rich, adored, quoted, industrious or disciplined, hasn't faced, at one time or another, the terror of not being able to write. There is nothing as devastating or debilitating as that hideous feeling. It's like taking a euphoric glider flight across wine country and then suddenly being flung from 20,000 feet without a parachute onto the terrain below, which has somehow turned to sheet rock.

I've been there. I've overcome it. I've been back and lived to tell about it and proudly show off the glorious pages of work I've done after the battles were over. If I can nurture myself through this agony, so can you.

Writer's block is caused by fear or anger or both. Every dry spell in my life can be traced back to one or the other. It's as though they go out for a drink and leave you there in a puddle of screaming mush wondering what the heck happened. You were doing so well this morning! You feel frantic, doomed. You are lost forever. You're never going to write again. Your only hope and salvation is a ''real'' job, with no demands. Just show up at nine, leave at five. Answer telephones, polish shoes, and that's it. You're not a writer. It's over. Forever. Amen.

Does any of that sound familiar? I bet it does. You might have seen me at the newsstand, searching seriously through the classified sections of seventeen daily papers, circling ads for clerk typists. Maybe you've seen me buying the G.R.E. study guide so I could go get an M.B.A. and have a real life. Or you saw me purchase a dozen ''how to'' books containing strategies on earning a million dollars a month on mail-order suppositories and software in my spare time. Sound familiar? Or did you perhaps catch my act as I grabbed copies of every magazine from *Barrons* to *The Singles Register* looking for a kind tycoon who'd take me off my own failed hands and marry me?

But I'm in good company. Every successful writer has crashed into this abyss. On bad days I can see the shadow of Oscar Hammerstein II across the street from me, climbing the oleander trees, preparing to jump in front of a big blue bus careening down the Berkeley Street hill. I think I've seen Shakespeare in a sweatsuit down at the park along the ocean ripping pages out of his notebook and muttering to himself like a bag lady. It's entirely possible for a songwriter who won a Grammy last year to be unable to write a note for the cleaning lady this week. Crazed, he grabs his award and heads for the trash bin. But a kid on a skateboard comes by whistling a tune our songwriter wrote and the crisis is over. A little recognition makes it all go away. The songwriter turns on his heels and runs to his piano, where he proudly places his Grammy again and begins to write a new song.

What would you do if you saw a barefoot, freckle-faced, four-year-old kid in a striped T-shirt and a Dodger cap sobbing on your doorstep as his ice cream falls into the street? You'd take him in. You'd want to comfort him. *I'd* want to hug him, rock him in my rocking chair, maybe lend him my teddy bear, kiss him on the forehead, hold his hand and tell him it's going to be okay. I'd buy him another ice cream cone—two scoops. I'd take him to a toy store and tell him he could have anything he wanted. Absolutely anything. I'd read him a wonderful story and tell him repeatedly how special he is. I'd pamper him. I'd protect him. I'd surprise him. I'd make this the best day of his life.

Each of us has a lost four-year-old inside of us making demands when we are blocked on what I call "midnight afternoons." Make a list of fifty things about this poor kid. Describe him or her in precise detail. Here are some questions to ask yourself to help get you started.

1. What color is his hair? Is it curly or straight?
2. What color are his eyes?
3. Is he crying?
4. Is he missing any teeth? Which ones?
5. Is he skinny? Chubby?
6. What language does he speak? Does he lisp?
7. What is he wearing? Describe his clothes in detail.
8. Did his mother abandon him?
9. Did an older kid steal his baseball cards?

10. Did another kid beat him up for his lunch money?
11. What can you do to make him feel better?
12. What can you do for him to surprise him and make this the most special and spectacular day of his life?
13. Will you take him to the beach or the ballgame?
14. Will you teach him to ride a bike or skateboard or fly an airplane?
15. Does he want a new daddy?
16. Does he want to sell you his sister?
17. Will he make you a package offer on his brother and sister?
18. Does he want a puppy? What kind? What will he name it?

Keep going. List fifty more things about this poor child. When you're finished, you'll see how needy this kid is and how terrific you can be to make it all up to him. That kid is you. So now take care of and comfort yourself just as you would the child. Make a list of twenty things you can do to pamper yourself. Then do them.

If you can learn to do that, you will learn how to take care of the frightened child inside you and make him feel safe again. People who feel safe can move on. They can take chances with blank pages. People who feel safe assume their ideas are good. People with good ideas write them down. People who write down good ideas keep finding better ones and eventually find a great one they want to run with. They nurture it. Structure it. Refine it. Rewrite it. They finish it. They reward themselves for that victory. Then they write something else.

GETTING READY TO WRITE

A lot of writers misinterpret their "prewriting" phase as being writer's block. They're simply getting ready to write. Any writer who wants to be good to himself has to learn to recognize his own personal, eccentric and often ridiculous warm-up.

Each of us has a pattern of preparing to write, and if you recognize that pattern you'll see you are making progress instead of thinking you're regressing. I used to get terribly upset with myself for not being able to take a beautiful, rhythmic, world-class tune and simply sit down to write the lyric. I had to do the following things first:

1. Plug in my heating pad and put it on my bed at precisely the right angle.
2. Arrange the pillows behind my back just so.
3. Get my thesaurus and rhyming dictionary.

4. Get comfortable with being in the room.
5. Get myself a cup of peppermint tea.
6. Get myself something to dunk in the tea.
7. Get myself another cup of tea that didn't have cookie dunk floating in it.
8. Find my other cassette player.
9. Find the tape containing the song to which I wanted to write a lyric.
10. Find my title notebook.
11. Find my current writing notebook.
12. Search for my gum.
13. Search for my lucky pen.
14. Make another cup of tea.
15. Rearrange the pillows.
16. Call everyone I knew on the planet and say I was going to write and ask them not to disturb me (even though I had an answering machine that could pick up on the first ring).
17. Put on my lucky lavender socks.
18. Go out in the rain with a ten-cent-off coupon to buy new tea bags on sale eighteen miles away.
19. Return home via a new route that took longer.
20. Boil the water for my new, bargain tea but decide on a diet soda instead.

I used to think that while I went through each of these steps I was not writing. I beat myself up for wasting all that time, which in some cases was as much as an hour or two. What I didn't realize until later was that all of those distractions were really part of my *warm-up* process. I needed to go through each of those steps before I was ready to write, before I felt safe enough and comfortable enough to take the risk and dig for something new.

I've worked hard to recognize changes in my warm-up process. And most of the time I have a pretty good grip on it. At one time I couldn't begin a project without a box of animal crackers handy. But some days I need french fries. There aren't any in my pantry. That means getting in my car and finding the nearest drive-through restaurant. At five in the morning they can be scarce. Nonetheless, as the menu changes, so do my writing and warm-up habits. Rather than saying I'm procrastinating and not doing what I should be doing (all those ugly words parents used on us), I've learned to understand what I am doing, to figure out why I'm doing it and realize that it's just part of the deal I made with myself in order to work.

In the case of the french fries, I finally realized that I needed to get out of the house for a little while before I started to work. I'm never not writing. I'm always getting *ready* to write. The semantics make a difference because one is a positive, nurturing statement; the other is punitive. So be careful how you phrase things. Learn to say them so they sound positive.

As an exercise, make a list of all the things you did before you last had a productive writing session. Don't leave anything out. Even making love or taking a shower or doing a pushup while making love in the shower or tweezing your eyebrows or brushing your teeth counts. So does vacuuming and gardening. And car washing, dental flossing, ironing, reading *Playboy* or *Playgirl* or both. Polishing your toe nails and eating sushi are also valid, although not necessarily in that order. Write down everything you did. This is not for publication. It is an exercise. It's therapeutic. Nobody but you will ever see it. So don't censor a single step. When you have your list, you'll see what you need to do to get ready to write. Do everything on that list, in order. I think you'll surprise yourself. You might just feel like writing.

But keep one important thing in mind. You didn't get blocked over night. And you might not get unblocked that quickly either. You have to work through it. Give yourself the time to do that. I know you're impatient and feel you have to get back to work. But if you really want to solve this problem, give it time. By putting too great a demand on this unblocking process, you're just creating a new series of frustrations.

I often find myself washing dishes before I start to write. I have a dishwasher, so why do I do this? Because the warm, soapy water feels good. It's very sensuous and at the same time safe, because I'm controlling the situation.

Another thing I've noticed I do now before starting to work is vacuuming. I have a housekeeper, so why do I do this? I like to see immediate, tangible results. And I do see them. The carpet is clean. The pile stands up straight. I did that. I controlled it. Now I can take charge of the thoughts and words lining up to pop out today.

FEAR

If you're stuck, make a list of things that frighten you. Or if you claim nothing does, then try a list of things that make you uneasy or uncomfortable or worry you a little. Things that might happen if the Big Earthquake comes or if the stock market crashes. Come on. You're a neurotic writer. Go for it. There must be something you're afraid of.

What about getting old? Or the perennial favorite, being alone forever and never achieving your songwriting goals? Does that strike any terror chords yet? Huh? Should I keep going or have I shaken you up enough to get you in touch with some of the things you really are afraid of? List them, in detail. Nobody will see this but you. Nobody's going to laugh at you or tell you you're imagining things.

Here are some suggestions to get you started:

1. Is there something you have to do that makes you a little uneasy?
2. Did somebody say something flippantly that caught you off guard and made you question your ability?
3. Do you think you've peaked?
4. Are you worried about earning a living?
5. Did someone imply you're just another writer and are in no way unique?
6. Did he say it in jest, but do you now wonder if he wasn't kidding?
7. Do you worry that your friends are doing better than you are?
8. If you're a writer with a contract or assignment, do you think they won't like what you hand in?
9. Do you think they'll buy you out of your contract and dump you?
10. Do you worry they'll hire someone younger and smarter in your place?

Now elaborate on what you're afraid of. Use scraps of paper if you want to. Or a fresh notepad. Or type it. Just list every detail of your deepest fears.

Then beside each item on your original list, write what you can do to remedy your fears. Your response to question three, for example, could be, "I'm writing better every day and I haven't peaked at all." A soothing response to question five would be that you're a very, very special writer and in spite of what someone might have said, you're a hit songwriter. Go down your list of fears and put a soothing comment next to each one.

There. You've faced it. It's not gnawing unseen and unknown in your gut anymore. You know now what you're up against. Now you can fight back using the soothing statements you've already written.

ANGER

If you're blocked and you're not afraid, then you're angry. It will help you get to the source if you ask yourself these questions:

1. Are you furious?
2. Totally aggravated?
3. Mildly disturbed?
4. Somewhat annoyed?
5. No? Not even with a neighbor who parks his car too close to yours and dings your fender?

Ahaaa! What are you mad at? Who are you mad at? What happened last week that still has you grinding your teeth? Maybe three months ago somebody said something and today you choose to address it. Do you see what I'm getting at? Things happen to us. As sensitive people we've developed mechanisms to cope with the things that happen to us. But they clog up our lives.

As with fear, you have to describe your anger. Pick up your pen and write down why you're mad. Write it in letter form if you choose—and pretend you're really going to mail it to the person you're mad at. You can use as many four-letter words as you want. You can forget punctuation and spelling, too. Tell everybody off. It's the best of all possible situations because you get to speak your mind and you're safe. Nobody can get even with you. If you don't want to write it down, talk it into a tape recorder and then play it back—loud. You are purging your soul.

People who are free of anger can feel gentle things. When you're happy you can let go and let other things happen to you. When you're not mad anymore, you have time to *feel* something else—to *do* something else. You can refocus your energy and find out what's going on in the world. Now you're open and receptive. You're curious about everything. You could just be reading the newspaper; an article might spark an idea for a song. You write the idea down in your notebook. You find another idea that goes with the first one. Pretty soon you have several ideas that could be included in a package. You get a title. You move the words around a little and you get a spectacular title. You write it down. You write it all down. You are writing again. *You are writing again!* You finish the song. You rewrite it your required number of times. You use it as proof that you can do it—and do it again!

Once, I was horribly blocked and in desperation went to Karin Mack, who gave a class at UCLA in overcoming writer's block. I learned the root of my problem was anger. I mean serious anger—leaking in from almost every aspect of my business and personal lives. Karin, who co-authored the excellent book *Overcoming Writing Blocks,* knew I was a songwriter. She suggested I go home and write a sonnet for each person or situation infuriating me. I should tell you that before I met Karin, I hadn't written a syllable in three months.

I went home and sat down at my kitchen table at 5 P.M. By midnight I'd written fifty-three sonnets. That's how mad I was. They weren't Shakespeare, you understand, but they were sonnets. I had no rules to follow other than to make each sonnet fourteen lines long and end with a rhyming couplet. Karin suggested the sonnet format since it was a *form,* and I was used to writing within certain guidelines. I was allowed to use four letter words. Yeah? Well, I was so riled I even made up new ones. The feelings I got down on paper were ones that I couldn't express to my publisher or my boyfriend. This sonnet outlet was perfect. I was surprised at how much anger there was inside me that was unexpressed. Occasionally a phrase popped out that was pretty good. So I purged my soul and at the same time regained my courage to create.

WARDROBE

When I write, I often wear an old sweatsuit, and by the end of the day there are cookie crumbs all down the front of it. My hair looks like it's been nuked and the mascara from the evening before is somewhere down around my nose. I might even have a hole in my "lucky lavender argyle socks." But on those days when I don't feel like writing or looking that unsavory, I wash my hair and style it perfectly, put on my going-to-tea-at-Trumps-makeup, try a new eye-shadow combination, unwrap a new pair of fancy pantyhose and put on the new outfit I'd been saving for a very special occasion. Then I make a deal with myself to go into my office. Just for five minutes. To tidy up papers. Before I know it I'm sitting at my desk, hard at work and loving it. What I do is make a happy occasion out of writing instead of the same old monotonous routine. Dressing up will work for you, too.

Whether you're blocked or simply have a long warm-up process, I hope you realize now that it's perfectly natural for you and all other successful writers to take side roads and detours to get to your writing. I don't care if you could've gone from A to B in three seconds. If you went from A to Z and then back to B, and B was successful, who cares about the trip to Z? Give yourself permission to have your warm-up time. Once you do, your writing will come a lot easier. You'll be in a much more positive frame of mind when you start, and that can only lead to more positive results.

PUBLISHING YOUR SONGS

MARKETING

Writing the song is only part of your job as a songwriter; I'd say it's 50 percent of the work. Others will argue with me and say it's as little as 10 percent. But whatever the percentage, your work has only just begun once the song is written. Now you have to get it on the radio. How do you do this?

First, test-market the song. Play it for several objective listeners for input to see if there are any glaring errors. An objective listener is someone who isn't automatically going to tell you it's great even if it isn't. He or she is someone who's knowledgeable about what's on the radio and who can constructively criticize your work.

You should develop a support group of other writers and musically inclined friends for whom you can play all your work on a consistent basis. Remember, you are writing because you want to share your songs with the world. The world will never hear them if you don't make your material accessible. You need constructive criticism all along the way. Believe me, it's better to get it before you demo the song than after, when you've spent days in the studio and hundreds or even thousands of dollars on a song that nobody is interested in.

Assuming there are just a couple of rough spots and you've taken the time to carefully rewrite the song to eliminate them, you are now ready for the next step: Making a demo.

THE DEMO

A demo is the recording you make to *demo*nstrate the song. With the easy access we all have these days to synthesizers that reproduce the sounds of every instrument, it's easy and practical to produce a full demo for just a little money.

Publishers and producers used to be content with a piano or guitar-voice demo. Now they've come to expect much more. Don't leave anything to their imaginations. Produce demos that can compete. Make yours as close to master-quality as you can—especially in R&B songs. As a case in point, the record of the song "Jump" used the demo instrumental track and just recorded the Pointer Sisters' voices over it. The writers were credited as co-producers of the record along with Richard Perry. This is getting to be more and more common. Publishers rarely spend money on demos anymore because so many writers have access to multi-instrumental-sounding synthesizers that create such good, inexpensive demos. I've been told repeatedly that publishers expect the demo to sound produced and slick by the time they hear the song. Then all they have to do is put their label on it and send it to a producer.

Remember: A synthesizer can enhance a song, but if the song isn't there to begin with, no amount of time at the studio console will help you. If a song doesn't "work" when whistled in the shower, it won't work with forty-eight tracks produced by Quincy Jones. It'll sound better, but it won't be a hit. And all he wants are hits. While some songs end up just being *album cuts,* no producer goes into a recording session without believing every song he has can be a *single.* You better realize that now, before you waste all your time on tedious and expensive demos that have no chance of making it to the radio. The bottom line, again, is to *write a great song* first. *Then* enhance it with all the rhythmic and technical doodads.

If you're a songwriter who does not sing at a professional, contemporary level, you should do some research before making your demos. First, gather a library of vocal tapes of singers who are available to make demos. Every songwriting association knows who these people are. Their newsletters and bulletin boards are full of ads placed by singers looking for work. Find at least ten voices you could use for your demos—ten voices that sound like the radio. Don't use "Broadway" voices, please—just pop, country or R&B. Remember: You want your songs to sound like those on the radio. You might think ten voices is overdoing it, but people in the music community are often on the road or tangled up in the dither of a million projects of their own in town. It's better to have several choices than to have only one acceptable singer who won't be available for weeks.

Never hire a singer to do a demo before you've heard him or her sing live or on tape. Ask each singer for references. Some great singers are so flaky they aren't worth the trouble. It takes a lot of work to coordinate a demo session, and you want to make sure the people you hire will show up—and on time. Time is money, especially when you're paying for studio time. Make sure yours is well spent.

Rehearse with the singer before the session. Find his or her key during the rehearsal. Make a chord chart—which could be as simple as a triple-spaced, typed lyric sheet with the chord names over the appropriate words. Have one chord sheet for each musician and singer, and one for the studio engineer.

If you aren't musical enough to produce the demo yourself, find one of those enterprising young musicians who can do it for you. Make a deal with him to hire the band, too. But don't hire him until you've heard samples of his work and have gotten references. It always comes back to equating your songs with your children. You wouldn't leave a child with a stranger, right? So neither would you turn your songs over to someone with whom you were totally unfamiliar.

Many of these demo wizards advertise in music newspapers and in songwriting association newsletters. They've got synthesizers that play drums, do background vocals and imitate the sounds of every instrument imaginable. As a result, they can offer you a good price on a demo package. But you want more than a good price. You want a great demo. Often a guy who only makes demos for a living just cranks out one after another and consequently they all sound alike. You didn't write your song to sound like everything else. Your song is unique. Your demo should be, too. Shop around. Find the right wizard.

While it's easier to find demo facilities in big cities, please, those of you who live in remote areas, *never send your song in the mail to be demoed.* Those mail-order places are usually schlock organizations. I can guarantee you'll be unhappy with the results. You'll be wasting your hard-earned money, and it'll make you angry and frustrated and reluctant to continue writing. You should be present at the recording session and feel free to give your input. After all, it's *your* song.

Don't bring a hundred friends, family and video cameras to the session. Come alone. This is business. Studio time is expensive. Musicians are artists and don't like a lot of people milling around telling them what to do. And besides, the inexpensive studios are usually small. The atmosphere there should be creative. Also, somebody has to be in charge. Decide that in advance of the session. Whatever you do, if you feel the tempo is wrong or the singer isn't emoting enough, speak up. Don't wait until the whole thing is over and it's too late to remedy the problem. It all boils down to taking charge of the recording process, not being victim to it.

You have to learn how to make demos, just as you have to learn to write. Each time out you'll be a little smarter. You'll become aware of how to cut corners and where time is best spent. Let me share a few anecdotes with you.

When I started to write, I was collaborating with Harriet Schock who later wrote "Ain't No Way to Treat a Lady." I was in Sherman Oaks and Harriet lived thirty miles away in Los Angeles. We were in a songwriting workshop together at Beachwood Music, and nobody on the planet earth was more motivated than the two of us were to make it as hit songwriters.

Twice a week, I'd come home from my social work job at the Los Angeles County Department of Public Social Services (I had an extensive file of unwed mothers, all of whom claimed the fathers of their babies were rock stars—so it *was* an "industry-related" job), gather up my reel-to-reel tape recorder, six-string guitar, twelve-string guitar, chord book, blank tapes and large bag of peppermints. Then I'd make the forty-five minute drive to Harriet's apartment.

Harriet was married then and her husband was our engineer. As a concession to him, we didn't take the phone off the hook while recording because he was always terrified his agent would call to offer him a "substantial role" in a movie. I'd hate to tell you how many interruptions we had—though never from theatrical agents. Harriet's husband had to drag the mattress off the bed and place it between Harriet and I in the living room, so that my guitar and Harriet's piano wouldn't leak onto each other's tracks. That's how we made our first demos. We didn't start off slick, believe me. Neither will you.

Another early writing partner of mine wrote lovely ballads, but at a time when everyone was looking for up-tempo bubblegum songs for wholesome, family-oriented groups with prepubescent male lead vocalists. My partner had a very determined backstage mother who believed in our ballads and wouldn't take no for an answer. Still, nobody wanted slow songs. They also didn't want girl singers, but my partner had a family friend who was a girl singer with a terrific voice who gave us a bulk rate on demos. So what we did was record our songs as ballads on my two-track tape recorder. Then I took the tape to a studio, where they sped up the tempo, making it sound "danceable." It also made the girl singer's deep, rich voice sound like a prepubescent male. That was the best we could afford in those days. It took time, but I learned—the hard way.

One last pointer on demos. While you will record in stereo, the true test of a recording is if it sounds good played mono on a small, terrible speaker. I was shocked to see a hit producer, who was a hero of mine, play back a terrific track he'd been recording and mixing for three days on a tiny, mono speaker box. He told me you can't rely on your audience's equipment being as good as what's in the studio. And it's true. If it works mono, it'll work stereo. The converse, however, is not true. So don't leave the studio until you listen to your song in mono.

CONTACTING PUBLISHERS

I'd like to open this section with a story. A music publisher and four friends who were not in the music business were out on a yacht in a choppy sea. The boat suddenly capsized in the storm. Sheldon the Shark came by and gobbled up four of the men instantly. The music publisher was untouched. When asked later by his fellow sharks why he let the music publisher go, Sheldon replied: "Professional courtesy."

This is how songwriters usually feel about music publishers. Actors have the same reaction to their agents. And it's a fact of life. We need each other and we hate each other. We don't think our publishers are doing enough. They think we're asking too much. They feel we're morons and envy our creativity and freedom, and we think that they've had lobotomies. Unfortunately, I doubt it's ever going to change, so get used to it.

Contacting publishers requires a lot of persistence. Music publishers are inundated with songs and overwhelmed by the demands made on their time from people they already know. So when you approach someone cold, be prepared for resistance. Don't take it personally. You can't be offended when someone who doesn't know you or your reputation doesn't jump. Accept their behavior as how they treat everybody and keep on trying.

Buy *Billboard* magazine. It is published weekly and lists all the hits on every chart—pop, country, gospel, R&B and video. Along with the title of each hit song, the name of the publishing company is listed along with the artists' and writers' names. So if you think your song is right for a particular group, find out who published their last hit and contact their publishing company.

If the group writes their own songs, don't bother submitting material there. They probably won't listen to outside material, let alone record it. Some artists are so lawsuit-prone, they're advised by their attorneys never to listen to anyone else's songs—especially someone they don't know.

So be smart about submitting material. Before you go to the trouble of trying to penetrate a busy publishing office, make sure all the acts they service aren't what we call "self-contained," recording songs they write themselves.

Assuming a group isn't self-contained, call the publisher of their latest hit and find out who their professional manager is. That's the guy who screens material. Check the correct address with the receptionist, telling her you need the information for your updated Rolodex. Then say goodbye. When you have a list of twenty professional managers and companies compiled, *then* start your serious calling.

Your initial call will go something like this:

RECEPTIONIST
(dithered)

Bigtime Music!

YOU
(charming)
Hi! Who is this I'm speaking to?

> RECEPTIONIST
>
> Why?

> YOU
>
> I'm a songwriter. My name is
> (fill in your name). What's yours?

> RECEPTIONIST
>
> Please hold.

You're on hold. Stay there. She'll be back. Eventually.

> RECEPTIONIST
> (still dithered)
>
> Bigtime Music! Hold on!

> YOU
>
> But . . .

Keep holding. Don't get mad. Stay calm. The little lady has all her lines flashing at once. Be her friend. She could use one.

> RECEPTIONIST
>
> Bigtime Music!

> YOU
> (quickly)
>
> Hi! I'm (fill in your name).
> And you are?

> RECEPTIONIST
>
> The receptionist.

> YOU
>
> Right. And a *very* good one. But
> what's your name? You have a lovely
> voice. I'd like to know who I'm
> speaking to.

> RECEPTIONIST
> (softening a little)
>
> Sherrysue. Please hold.

And you do. You're at a pay phone and it's starting to rain. But do not leave your post.

RECEPTIONIST

Bigtime Music!

YOU
(quickly)

Hi Sherrysue. It's me (fill in
your name). I'm a songwriter. I
have a hit for Kenny Rogers. Nobody
else in town has heard it yet.
Since I see in *Billboard* that your
company published Kenny's last single,
I'd like to meet with (the professional
manager) and see if we can do business
together and make some money.

RECEPTIONIST

Can you hold?

You're dying to strangle the woman, but you keep your cool. You need
her. There's a line of tattooed, toothless truckers behind you waiting to
use the phone. But you don't give up now. Finally . . .

RECEPTIONIST

Yeah?

YOU

Sherrysue, like I said, I've
got a *hit* song right here for
Kenny Rogers and—

RECEPTIONIST

We don't listen to unsolicited
material.

YOU
(confidently)

Hey—I know. But this isn't just
another unsolicited tune. I met
(professional manager) at a seminar
a few weeks ago and she asked me to call
as soon as I had something on tape.
I'm a professional songwriter, Sherrysue,
and I'd like your help and cooperation
in putting me through to (professional manager).

RECEPTIONIST
He's in a meeting.

YOU
When could I call back?

RECEPTIONIST
He's going to New York tonight for
two weeks.

YOU
Okay. I'll give you a call a few
days after he gets back.

RECEPTIONIST
But then he's going to Guam and Helsinki . . .

Although you want to put your fist through the phone booth door, you bite your tongue, take a very deep breath and cheerfully say you'll call back again. And you do.

In my eight-session songwriting course, three of the lessons are devoted exclusively to handling people on the phone. It's an art. Work on your telephone craft as much as you do your writing. It's a big part of your job. You've already worked hard and sacrificed a lot to create those great songs of yours. Don't they deserve that extra push to get them heard? Call the Sherrysues of the world back. Keep leaving messages for the professional managers. And since they probably won't return your calls, you keep calling them. Eventually they'll crack and ask you to send in a tape. But don't do that. Push for a face-to-face meeting. Otherwise your song will be listened to on the run in a stack of a thousand and will have no chance whatsoever. You didn't come this far to get a form rejection letter.

So work on your telephone persona. It should not be the same person who created the songs, but someone you put on, like a brand-new, smartly tailored suit. Your business persona is irresistibly persuasive, charming, assertive *and* persistent without ever being obnoxious. Work on this persona until you've got your "act" down.

You might even want to give yourself another name while you're making your business calls. When I'm feeling too vulnerable to call as Molly because of some past difficulty with a particular person, I call as "Sally," my assistant. Nothing they say about Molly or about being too busy to speak to Molly ruffles my feathers. I am gracious, understanding, and I always get what I want. Sally has no emotional investment in the business at hand and can take as much rejection as anyone can dish out. She's cool. She's calm. Above all else, she is professional. When you can behave in a totally professional way, you will triumph on the telephone.

POWER PHONING

Developing confidence on the phone requires practice. As an exercise, try calling the chief executive officer of a major corporation. Say you have an idea for his corporation which will make a lot of money. See how far you get and how many underlings try to intercept you en route. Remember, you have nothing personal at stake here. Your only goal is to reach the CEO. He doesn't know you. But you must speak to him to complete this exercise. Once I got the highest-ranking general in the Air Force to call me back. After that, I realized it couldn't be all that difficult to get through to a publisher at Warner Brothers Music. I want you to feel that confident, too.

PREPARING FOR A PUBLISHING MEETING

Let's assume that after calling back twenty times and insisting (without threatening to slash the tires of his Porsche) that the professional manager make an appointment to see you, you've arranged to meet him at his office. Prepare a cassette on which there are no more than three songs. The tape should be "cued up" and in the correct consecutive order on your cassette tape. Please don't go on safari through a ninety-minute cassette for a song while in a publisher's office. Don't bring him a broken tape or a bad copy with a long explanation, either. Neatly type all your lyric sheets. Put your name, phone number and the name of the other writer(s) at the top of the page and write the following at the bottom of the sheet:

© (Year) Your Name.

And that's all. Don't write "Member of ASCAP" or "Member of Texas Music Association" or "Runner-up in the Wyoming Watusi Festival 1945." It reeks of amateurishness. Please—just put the information I suggested.

While this might appear inconsequential, one client approached me with her lyrics typed on a typewriter that had fancy script type. It was impossible to read because the printing was so small. It was also so curlycued I couldn't have deciphered it even if the letters were bigger. This is not an invitation to the cotillion you're submitting. It is a product with which you're hoping to convince someone in power to do business with you. A publisher is in business to make money. You should present yourself and your work as though you are, too.

The same is true for cassette labels. They should bear your name, your phone number and the titles of your songs. They should not have adorable, fluorescent silver and gold notes dancing all over the label or little treble clefs breaking out between the words. Less is more.

You should also have a business card that bears your name, the word "songwriter" after your name, a phone number on which there is an answering service, your address and that's all. No cute, smiling notes or darling little treble clefs here, either. Spend your money on a good demo—not on a fancy card.

Don't leave a business card that lists some other profession, even if you're a United States senator, an astronaut or a Los Angeles Ram. Your card should simply tell the publishers that you are a songwriter and here's where they can reach you.

The former vice president of music for Lorimar had the most ridiculous business card taped to his desk for all visitors to see. It said "John Jones. Motion Pictures, Spare Ribs. The Best of Both." Let me assure you, I wouldn't call him for either.

You can order attractive, succinct business cards at an instant-printing place for $20. There should be room on your card to put a quarter (a twenty-five-cent piece) that wouldn't cover any writing. That means a lot of blank space. People resist reading too many tiny words. Keep this in mind when you have your cards printed.

Dress in what I call "power clothes." They give you a strong, dynamic, magnetic presence in public. Have you ever noticed there are some people you turn and watch as they walk by? There's something about them that exudes confidence. You should be one of those people, whether you're a man or a woman.

I have special "power clothes" I wear just to meetings. They're carefully coordinated in colors that suit me best. My shoes are "showroom new" and well taken care of. My hair and makeup are perfect and my jewelry—even if it's just a watch—is carefully selected to tell the person I'm meeting that I've got it all together, I'm hip, I'm artistic and I'm unique. You should make the same presentation for yourself. It might take some shopping to find ensembles that feel both comfortable and "powerful" at the same time. But get used to wearing these new clothes and to acting "as if" in them. Then when you really do have a meeting, you'll be confident and ready.

I'd make a point of finding out in advance the kind of clothes the professional manager wears. The odds are he's hip-looking, possibly dressed like nobody you've ever seen before on the planet. I don't know if we're talking orange and purple spikes, but up-and-comers in the music business like to fit in. They often idolize rock stars and dress to imitate them.

If you'd normally wear a conservative three-piece suit to a business meeting, here's where your wardrobe has to be changed. A guy showing up in that outfit will be labeled "a suit" and will be seen as an outsider by everyone in the company. Even the staff lawyer at A&M wears a promotional T-shirt like everybody else. So check out the hip men's and women's "looks" and try to find one in which you are comfortable.

While I wouldn't suggest you spike your hair for the meeting, be aware that you should try to look as hip as possible to *mirror* the person with whom you're having the meeting. If you do, he'll feel more comfortable with you. And that will make it easier for him to like you and your songs.

Be on time. If you've never been to the office before, allow time to get lost. The receptionist is going to be just as hassled in person as she was on the phone. The last thing she needs is a yahoo on her hands who's late and flustered.

While I wouldn't go so far as to suggest you bring the receptionist a rose, I would strongly recommend you make a good impression on her while you're waiting for the meeting with her boss. Ask her a lot of questions about herself. Chances are nobody cares about her in the company. They think of her as a blob with black fingernails who answers the phone. So she'll be flattered by your interest in her. And let's keep that professional. Maybe she's a songwriter, too. Or a singer. Maybe she loves music and is a serious groupie. Or maybe she's just out of school and will one day be president of a major record label. She'll also know the gossip about who's cutting what and the kinds of songs that are in demand that week.

Find out what her story is. The chances are good that in three to six months she'll be working somewhere else, doing something similar or a step up from what she's doing now. If you already have a positive, professional relationship with her, then you'll have an ally wherever she goes. So while you're waiting, be sure to thank her for putting together this meeting. That way she'll feel important and will remember you for it.

THE MEETING

Start the meeting by shaking hands. Ladies, too. No wimpy handshakes, please. This is business. Even if the atmosphere doesn't reflect it—music is blaring and mohawk haircuts are manifesting themselves up and down the halls—this is still a business meeting. The executive preamble that would occur if you were selling lumber or life insurance is appropriate.

Make the publisher feel comfortable. You'd expect it to be the other way around, but it isn't. The first few seconds aren't about music at all, but about sizing each other up to see if you are going to establish a positive and fertile ground for a business relationship. Start by giving him a compliment on a piece of art or a photograph of a child or even an item of his clothing. "Gee, I love that poster." "What a darling child. Is he yours?" These are ways of saying you like and admire him.

Right now the publisher has the power and you want his approval. But don't let him know how much you need it. Act as if this is just another meeting for you. Assume the attitude that you have lots of important people interested in your songs. You've *chosen* to have this meeting with him. Be sure he doesn't know you're seeing him just because nobody else would return your calls.

You want to make a strong connection with the publisher, because you'll be writing songs for a long time. You'll want to come back with your new ones. Flaky, acned, knock-kneed stockboys grow up to be presidents of record companies. Your job is to make sure that when they move up, you move up with them.

Assuming your opening remarks go well, get right into your pitch. Tell the publisher you're a good songwriter. You've studied the craft of writing, you have "holds" on your material by a couple of major publishers and you've heard good things about his particular energy and way of doing business. You want to work with him because you know you can make a lot of money together. You've also heard that in addition to his being a good businessman and up on everything going on in the industry, he's very sensitive. So you feel he will be able to connect with your material.

Then you play your tape. He may not like the first song. Don't get flustered. Ask him to fast forward the tape to the next tune. If he doesn't like that one either, don't be thrown. Ask him to suggest how you could rewrite it to make it more commercially accessible. Now he's involved with the material. He feels a connection to it—and to you.

Then comes a crucial part of the meeting. It's the time when you have to separate yourself as creator of the songs from the one who is doing the business of marketing them. If the publisher doesn't like your present work but offers an explanation, listen to him. Tell him you hadn't thought of that before, say he's given you some terrific ideas, you appreciate his input and you hope to see him again soon because he's been a big help to you. Now that you know his tastes in music a little better, you'll be back when you have these songs rewritten or when you have some new material that falls more into the categories he is most comfortable representing.

If he takes a phone call or a series of phone calls or suddenly needs to look at a magazine, don't take it personally. All publishers do that. I think it's a test. One guy answered five calls while I was attempting to play him a song—a song I'd rewritten four times at his request for no money. I finally mustered the courage to ask him to please hold his calls until I was finished, which would only be two minutes. He said he absolutely couldn't do that because he was in the midst of a big soundtrack deal. I shrugged and went on with my song. However, the *next* time I had a meeting with this man, I walked into his office and he told his secretary to hold his calls. So it was a test. Be aware of the dynamic and act accordingly.

Anna Hamilton Phalen, a successful screenwriter, was once trying to tell a story to a development executive at a movie studio, who suddenly picked up a basketball, bounced it a few times on the rug, threw it up in the air for a while and then tossed it to poor Anna who was in the middle of her pitch. The ball went back and forth between "the players" while Anna tried to maintain some order and passion in her presentation. I know Anna to be assertive and capable of asking someone not to throw things at her—whether she's telling stories or not—but there was something terribly intimidating about this meeting and this particular development guy that prevented Anna from speaking up. So she became the victim.

On hearing this story, I asked Anna what she felt she could've done in retrospect to stop the "basketball game" and regain control of the meeting. I suggested she could've tossed the ball into the garbage pail. But Anna said she should have kept it, twirling it on the end of her finger for a few minutes like Magic Johnson. I felt she would've made her point with just a little more impact if the finger that was twirling the ball had a perfectly manicured nail at its end.

In retrospect, we were both able to see that the whole thing was a power play. We laugh at it now. But it is unconscionable that a highly professional, successful writer had to suffer like that. When this happened, Anna wasn't some unknown off the bus from Cupcake, Kansas, either. She wrote the script for *Mask,* which had just been released. The film got rave reviews. People were all over Anna like bad suits trying to get her to *come* to meetings. So it wasn't that she was unknown or uncredited. People who hold meetings are often horribly rude. You can't—absolutely cannot—take their behavior personally.

When your meeting is over, shake hands, thank the receptionist by name for her help, leave unobtrusively and don't fall apart until you're out of the building.

Be sure you do something terrific for yourself as a reward for having had the courage and stamina to get through that meeting. This "gift"— a bouquet of flowers, a box of Jujubes, a movie, a nice dinner at your favorite restaurant, a night with Zena the Zebra lady or Mr. July—will give you more leverage with your sensitive, creative self when you have to set up and go to the next meetings.

After you've taken care of yourself, then you have to rally your objectivity. Write the publisher a personal note, thanking him for his very good suggesions. Say you'll give him the first chance to listen to your next few songs. This personal note should be handwritten on nice stationery. The publisher will no doubt be impressed with it. He spends his life under the gun from people who are usually frantic, uneducated, speak in monosyllabic grunts and have never heard of Emily Post. This publisher will remember you for treating him with respect and good taste, because that makes him feel like he has some social graces, too.

Now let's assume you've gotten over the rejection from the meeting. You've battled with your ego and have decided to try rewriting the songs. Either that or you're content to let the old ones be for the time being, learn from them and start fresh with some new material. When it's ready to be shown, contact the publisher again.

Call your old friend Sherrysue. Remind her about the great meeting you had with her boss a couple of weeks earlier. Tell her you have some new material and the publisher asked to hear it as soon as it was on cassette. This second appointment should be easier to set up, but it might require as much persistence as the first one did. You don't know what crises may have befallen the company that morning. So don't take it personally if the publisher does not call you back. In a place where six stereos are constantly blaring six different songs, each vying for domination, there are lots of distractions. Keep calling. And keep your cool.

If you still can't get through, try another personal note. Be pleasant, and mention that you've tried to reach him, you have a new song as promised and you hope when his desk is clear the publisher will find a few minutes to see you. That usually works for me. In the meantime, while you're waiting for him to respond, call twenty other publishers. I always feel best when I have many options open to me. It's not fair to yourself to let one person's decision to take or not to take your call determine your value as a person or as a writer. But it's hard to separate his not calling you back, for whatever reason, from a personal rejection.

So set up lots of meetings. Assume you've got good songs and you're someone the music publishing world is lucky to be doing business with. Decide ahead of time you won't allow anyone's jammed schedule to get you down or stop your creative flow. When you put out good, gracious, businesslike energy, it'll eventually be returned in kind.

POWER PACKAGE

One way around the difficulty of presenting what I call "orphan songs" to a music publisher is to have your own group. I feel that any songwriter starting out now has to be acutely aware of the state the music business is in. More and more artists are recording their own songs. Look at the Hot 100. Niney-nine of these tunes are "self-contained," which means that you and everybody else who writes are trying to get material to the same one percent. Self-contained groups have producers, friends or relatives who write. Many of them also have contractual obligations to music publishers. So your chances with them are slim to none.

So create your own vehicle for your songs. Make a deal with a hot but still unknown group you can work with to write for or with them. Be sure they are contractually bound to keep their commitments to you. In writing. Then you can approach any publisher with a "package"—you and someone to sing your songs. Now that you've presented the publisher with an artist, you've just eliminated the hardest part of his job. Now he can help you get the artist or group a record deal. And then you're on your way.

If you don't know anybody who sings or performs, go out and find someone who does. Search local clubs, high school bands and talent contests. Be objective. Don't just settle for the local piano teacher or the first cute guy with a good voice who bops along on a designer skateboard. Listen to the radio. Go to concerts. See what's selling. Find an artist or a group that can realistically compete in the current marketplace. It'll require a lot of work, but you owe it to your songs. You want them on the air. This is the quickest and most hard-nosed, realistic way to get them there.

My own experience has shown me repeatedly that just when I've given up on ever hearing from a particular person and have moved on to someone else, that's when the first guy calls me back. I'm inevitably in the shower washing my hair. Of course, I can't tell the publisher this. I let the lather drip into my eyes while I talk business. The publisher will usually apologize for not getting back to me sooner. My job, and now yours, is to make him feel at ease again. You tell him right up front you weren't worried about your project so much as you were concerned about him and hoped everything was all right. He'll appreciate your concern, and he'll be able to tell that you're a serious, business-minded person.

POWER LUNCH

Tell the publisher you'd like to take him to lunch. It's always better to meet a busy man out of the office, away from ringing telephones. No matter how crowded his schedule, he'll still have time to eat. If he isn't free for three weeks, fine. You'll wait. Set a date.

Lunch is a social occasion, but business creeps in and gets taken care of anyway. And treating someone to lunch or a drink makes it *your* occasion. It gives you power points and makes the other person feel pampered and important. So everybody wins.

Here are a couple of pointers on lunch that work for me. First, ask your guest's secretary where her boss likes to eat. Make a reservation. Arrive early and make sure your table is ready. Ask to be seated. Choose the "power seat," which enables you to see everything that is going on in the room but restricts your lunch partner's view to you.

I realized how important this is when it happened to me by accident. I was lunching with a producer at MGM. He was being particularly helpful, offering a constructive critique of a film musical project I'd spent a year writing. I felt I needed all the help I could get. As the producer talked, I noticed out of the corner of my eye that Bo Derek was sitting at the next table. Luckily my producer didn't see her, because I was strategically placed in the "power" seat. The producer kept on about my project and I wrote down everything he said. When our lunch was over (I had great notes, just as I hoped I would), the producer stood up, saw Bo, and that was the ballgame. I didn't exist anymore. Neither did my screenplay. He was totally distracted and couldn't put a sentence together. So although the location of my seat that particular day was just a lucky accident, from that time forward I've always tried to ensure myself the power seat in any lunch or dinner meeting to avoid wasting it on distractions—Bo or otherwise.

After your guest arrives, ask him what he's going to order and request the same thing. More mirroring. If he wants a pizza with everything on it and you order a watercress salad, it'll make him feel like a slob. So whatever he's having, you're having, even if you hate it. Keep the

lunch social. Ask him about himself. He probably has some great stories. Everybody does. I'm sure he'll be flattered by your interest. In his
business, nobody cares much about him—just what he can do for them.
So this is a nice bonding time for the two of you.

Even though he may have an expense account and can write off the
lunch, don't let him. You take care of the check. The one who pays the
bill has the power. You're this close to getting it—go the rest of the way
and grab it.

Assuming a publisher likes one of your songs and wants to publish it,
you should know how to proceed. First, never negotiate your own
deals. Writers are too close to their work to be objective about its value.
Have a music attorney act on your behalf. (I'm sure if Little Richard had
it to do over again, he'd certainly hire a lawyer to represent his publishing contract.)

The first thing attorney Jay Cooper told me when he negotiated my
first staff-writing deal was that nothing is standard. Publishers might tell
you they're giving you a standard contract so you'll sign it quickly, but
everything is negotiable—including the term of the agreement, which
could be from six months to forever, and the royalty rate paid on sheet
music, which ranges from nine cents to a quarter per copy sold. The
royalty rate on record *sales* is uniform, with the writer(s) and publisher
sharing five cents per copy. For writers who record their own material,
however, record companies pay sales royalties, known as "mechanical
royalties," at a reduced rate. Publishing agreements can get complicated, so I strongly recommend you invest in a good attorney who will
explain your contract to you. In addition to being able to negotiate from
an objective position (because he didn't write the song, he's just representing the writer), a good attorney can get you a better deal simply
because of his reputation. If Ross T. Schwartz or some other top music
attorney tells a publisher he's representing you, the publisher will automatically have more respect for you and the value of your work than if a
personal-injury lawyer from Des Moines calls him on your behalf.

The writer(s) and publisher of a song are partners. Each gets 50
percent of the royalties. Whether there are three or thirty writers on a
song, they all share 50 percent of the income, while the publisher still
gets his half. The publisher is like your agent. He represents you and the
song. His job is to get your material to an artist who will record it and
make you all a lot of money. Therefore, a good publisher must know
who's looking for songs, which artists sell the most records, and how to
make the most money in the short run and the long run, too. A song that
is a hit this year could currently earn its writer and publisher $100,000 a
year, every year, until the copyright expires. A good publisher will

constantly explore new ways for your songs to make money. He'll find new artists to re-record old songs. He'll get your songs in movies and on Muzak. He'll arrange licensing agreements to use your hit song for a commercial. A good example is "Through the Years," a hit for Kenny Rogers now used for a Volvo commercial. "Unforgettable" was a hit in the forties and is now heard in a donut commercial. The licensing fees these songs command are astronomical. A good publisher will make sure your songs are constantly re-marketed to produce as much income as possible.

Sometimes a publisher will give you a small advance against future royalties. This could range from $100 to as much as $10,000, depending on the song and the track record of the writers. Often, the publisher lays out the cost of making the demo and considers this your advance. I'd always have your lawyer request an advance, because a publisher will rarely, if ever, volunteer one. Also, be sure you're clear on the duration of the contract. According to the copyright law, the period for which you receive royalties on a song is the duration of the life of the writer plus fifty years. But you have to negotiate up front how long the publisher gets to keep his publishing share of your song.

Try to get a reversion clause in your contract. This means that if after a specified length of time the song hasn't been recorded, it will revert back to you. Publishers are often reluctant to include reversion clauses because it can take a long time to get a song recorded and *released*. An artist might cut twenty songs for an album but only need ten. If your song turns out to be one of the ten that didn't make it to the album, there is a chance the song might come out on the next album. And that could be a year away or longer. Artists can be dropped from their record labels. Maybe their new labels want to start over with fresh material, cut by another producer. In that case, they wouldn't want the songs left over from the early albums and "in the can." But sometimes there's a little gem of a song that sits quietly in the can and is suddenly released as a single because tastes change and so do song styles. That happened to Steve Dorff and me with "Let Me Love You Once Before You Go." Our song was originally recorded on a Barbara Fairchild album that was never released. Two years later, Columbia decided to release the album with our song as the single. It was a big hit. So you never know what can happen down the road. That's why publishers are reluctant to include reversion clauses. If my publisher had allowed "Let Me Love You Once Before You Go" revert back to Steve and me, he'd have done all the work of getting the song recorded for nothing. He'd have lost out because of the two-year time lapse. Publishers can only pitch songs to artists and producers. They can't control the *release* of albums. That's their argument against reversion clauses.

I always ask for that clause, however, and the following story illustrates why. Early in my career, when I hadn't had any meaningful records yet and nobody knew who I was, I wrote a song that was published by a major music publisher. Since they wouldn't give me an advance, they gave me a one-year reversion clause instead. If they wanted to keep the song beyond that year, they agreed in our contract to pay me $150. Although they pitched the song everywhere, when the year was up, nobody had recorded it. So I asked the president of the company if he was still interested in keeping the song. He was. I asked him when I could expect my $150 pick-up payment. He said that while the company put the clause in my contract, they didn't really *do* that anymore and didn't want to pay me. I was anxious for him to have the song if he felt he could get it cut, but at the same time, we had a deal. I said if he didn't want to pay me, he'd have to return the song. At that time, $150 was a windfall for me. But the president told me clearly that he didn't want to "throw good money after bad," and gave me back my song.

Nine months later, I signed a staff-writing deal with Almo Music and became a salaried employee in exchange for giving them the publishing rights to all the songs I wrote during a one-year period. Since the song in question had reverted back to me at the end of its year at the other publishing company, I assigned the copyright to Almo Music, my new publisher, and rewrote it. It got cut right away. A year later, my song "Silver Wings and Golden Rings" won an ASCAP Country Music Award for being one of the most performed songs of the year. What made that success even sweeter was at the awards banquet, I was seated next to the man from the first publishing company who had originally told me the song wasn't worth $150. That night he graciously toasted me and confessed he should never have let the song go. But that reversion clause made my career. Be sure *you* don't leave any songs behind if you can help it.

INSIDE A MUSIC PUBLISHING HOUSE

In fairness to the hand that feeds me, I called Brenda Andrews, who was my publisher at Almo Music and is now vice president of the company. I told her I needed some input from the other side of the desk.

Brenda is proof that my Sherrysue theory is correct, although Brenda is completely professional and always has been. Eighteen years ago she had a deadly straight job in an insurance company. Her gig was to shut up and just do it. A friend of hers who worked at A&M knew Brenda was looking for a job and told her about a receptionist opening in the publishing division. "Oh no . . ." was Brenda's reply. But something made her go for an interview.

At the time, the company was young. There were only sixty-two employees. Brenda met with Chuck Kaye, who was head of the publishing division. He liked Brenda immediately but wondered why she'd want to leave the security of an insurance company to come work for him. She said she was choking to death. So he offered her the job. He did say, however, that it only paid $105 per week. "Oh no . . ." Brenda replied. "I'm getting $110 now." They went back and forth a while on that one. According to Brenda it was like bleeding a turnip. But when the negotiations ended, Brenda had her other $5 and Chuck had himself one sharp receptionist.

Working her way through the ranks, Brenda moved up from receptionist to copyright clerk to secretary to executive secretary. She longed to become a professional manager, but half-chauvinistic, half-protective Chuck Kaye said the street was no place for a woman. But when Chuck left the company to try the good life on a yacht in Hawaii, Brenda went to work for the new director of publishing. One day, while producer Tom Catalano was waiting to see him, Brenda slipped Tom a tune for Helen Reddy. It was a song called "Long Hard Climb," written by Ron Davies, an A&M staff writer. The tune was cut and became the title of Helen's album—one of a long series of platinum discs Tom produced for her. Brenda got a $250 bonus and has never been so pleased with herself.

When the directorship of the publishing wing changed hands and flamboyant Artie Wayne took over, he promoted Brenda to professional manager at last. She continued moving up—to coordinator of creative affairs and then director of creative affairs. In 1980, with Chuck Kaye out of the water and back at the helm, Brenda was promoted to vice president. That day Chuck told her, "No one can ever take this away from you," and no one has.

I asked Brenda what she'd suggest to someone who was starting out in the music business. Her first suggestion was to "get outta Dodge." By that she means there's no way you can be in the music business long distance—through the mail or visiting a music city twice a year for a week. You have to *live* in one of the music cities—L.A., Memphis, San Francisco, Nashville, New York, or Minneapolis (which is Prince's home town).

Brenda went on. "You have to compete in the big pond. It's no good being number one in Wyoming. The true test is L.A. You have to be a contender there if you ever hope to win. It takes a lot to leave home, but you have to do it. You need the experience. You have to go to clubs and see what's out there. If you're an artist, get on the bills on talent nights. Showcase yourself. In a music city. Not in Bountiful, Texas. Nobody will ever find you there. The mountain doesn't come to Mohammed.''

Brenda says they don't have the studios or the technology to help a writer produce a competitive sound in small towns. She's heard tapes from Chicago, Detroit and Dallas, but they all sound dated. If those writers were living in L.A., they'd hang out with writers and publishers and artists and bands who were hip. They'd have meetings with people in the business who know what's hot. They'd adapt their styles to the changing times. Brenda feels that that's impossible to do from a non-music city, because by the time a sound or a feel gets that far, it's old and has already been replaced with something more current that you don't know about yet.

A&M does not accept, nor will it ever accept, unsolicited tapes. The main reason is this: fear of lawsuits. Brenda said that although they won a suit filed against "I Know I'll Never Love This Way Again," written by Will Jennings and Richard Kerr and recorded by Dionne Warwick, it still cost A&M over $60,000 to defend itself against an amateur who claims he submitted that same song—unsolicited—to the company. Since then, no material has been accepted in that manner. And Brenda says there's no way that's ever going to change.

So how does a newcomer on his way up get to meet Brenda Andrews and her colleagues? How do you break through that hard "no"? Brenda speaks on panels at seminars—and has a deep personal commitment to black music seminars in particular. She goes to industry dinners. She attends industry functions. A gracious and gregarious lady by nature, Brenda says if someone approaches her in a businesslike manner outside the office, she'll suggest he or she send a tape marked to her personal attention, indicating in a note the circumstances under which they were introduced. "It's a business of contacts. It's a clique. Very clannish. You have to know people to meet people. That's how it is, and it's not going to change."

Brenda admits deals are often made over cocktails, on the golf course or the tennis court. Writers put you in touch with other writers who introduce you to publishers. Or lawyers with good connections will listen to your tape and make a call to someone of Brenda's stature. But she won't—no she *can't*—listen to anything submitted any other way. Period. Brenda is a vice president of a major music publishing company with 320 employees. If she says you have to hang out and get to know the folks, you better believe her. She's learned from eighteen years in the trenches what the facts are.

Once you've introduced yourself to a publisher, lawyer or producer at an industry function or social occasion, then you can proceed to call him, even if the company doesn't take unsolicited material.

Brenda says that although it's a closed, clannish business, she knows the value of new blood and is quick to encourage new talent. It's a company's responsibility to nurture and develop new acts. New acts need new songs, new sounds.

I asked Brenda to imagine she had a magic wand that she could wave to change the music business anyway she wanted to. What would she do?

1. She'd allocate more funds for record companies to develop new artists and writers.

2. She'd have more black producers working with white artists— instead of white producers working with black artists, the way it usually is now.

I watched as Brenda filled her briefcase with cassettes and said good-night to Winkie, her delightful and highly efficient assistant. We walked out together, down the hall lined with gold records. "Going to hear somebody sing?" I asked as she got into her car. "No way. This is Wednesday. Wednesday nights I go to church. Without that, there wouldn't be any hit songs for anybody."

If you were smart, you'd join her church choir.

MAKING MONEY IN
THE MEANTIME

Although the "struggling artist" has been romanticized in movies and books, it's no fun being poor. I was. I don't recommend it. Not having income puts tremendous pressure on you to make money quickly with your writing. That isn't fair to you. You should be writing songs to express yourself, to share your feelings with the world. Don't put the demand of financial survival on your songwriting too early or it could squash your chances forever. I don't know any great songwriter who has lasted who writes just for the money.

While the ultimate goal for most songwriters is a smash hit played once an hour for six months on eight thousand radio stations across the country (plus an equal amount in the rest of the world), there are ways of earning substantial income using songwriting skills but aiming at less competitive and more lucrative short-run markets.

The first thing you must know is never to take no for an answer. Ever. Write that a hundred times a day and repeat it to yourself while you're soliciting work. If somebody turns you down, learn why, change your pitch a little and go back again with a new angle. Success is contagious. You'll see how people who've dismissed you as a hack suddenly love you when you've been successful elsewhere.

WARNING

You never sell your songs. Never. You have them *published.* When that occurs, you receive fifty percent of the income from the songs. Even though a publisher may give you a cash advance against future royalties from the song, you still have not *sold* the publisher your work. You will always receive the writer's share of the income derived from that song. Even if someone offers you a million dollars to buy your song outright, never do it. If you have a hit this year, it could earn you $100,000 per year every year for the rest of your life—and make the same amount for your estate for another fifty years after your death. So songs are *not* for sale. Only the publishing rights are. Unfortunately, there are shysters out there who prey on inexperience in the music business. Let me give you an example. In the fifties, Little Richard was just a naive kid from the backwoods when an unscrupulous weasel came along, had him sign on the dotted line and gave him $10,000—more than the young singer/songwriter could possibly imagine having in three lifetimes. What Little Richard didn't realize until later was that because he was so hungry for success and because $10,000 seemed like such a windfall to him at the time, he didn't read the contract carefully or have it reviewed by a reputable attorney. That $10,000 was *all* the income Little Richard ever saw from those copyrights. He should have received royalties for all his hits—"Long Tall Sally," "Slippin' and Slidin'," "Lucille," "Rip It Up," "Ready Teddy," "Tutti-Frutti," "Good Golly Miss Molly"—plus many other songs that he wrote and recorded. Now he is suing his publisher for $50,000,000. So *never sell your songs.*

You should also *never give anybody money to record your songs.* There are vanity recording companies run by song sharks stashed away in post-office boxes across the country. These people know how hard it is for a writer or artist to make a deal through normal music-business channels. They promise to record and release your songs and maybe even get them played two or three times on a local station. They charge you from $500 to $10,000 to make a record and will even send you sample copies with your picture on them. But nothing ever comes of this. They are simply preying on your ego and counting on your impatience. *They are in business to rip you off.* Sure, you get your song or your album recorded, but by musicians who crank out fifty songs a day, making them all sound alike. These companies never have national distribution or legitimate connections with meaningful radio stations. A legitimate record company pays *you* royalties. So *never send anybody money to record your songs. Ever.*

JINGLES

While you're learning the business of music and are slowly building credibility and contacts, write jingles. Try a local store or business.

Offer to write a jingle for free. You need the credit and the reputation of being able to deliver. Good news travels fast. Figure you'll get paid for the next gig. From there you could move up to a national account and get residuals. That's fine. We'll take it. Your jingle could play for years. Sometimes commercials become hits—like "We've Only Just Begun" and more recently "The Pride is Back." That's okay. We'll take that, too. Any success on this level will give you the luxury of having time to write the songs you really want to write.

Most jingle writers have a "reel" containing samples of their work. You'll need one, too. If you don't have one, write a couple of jingles to showcase yourself. Take nationally advertised products like Coca-Cola, Ford and McDonald's and write something new for each account. Produce a professional-sounding demo and use it as a calling card for your first jingle gig. That shows a lot of moxie. People in that business respect it. Play the game by their rules.

Most developing writers have been rejected so often and are so anxious to have their work recognized that when someone does want their material, they are eager to give it away. In the case of jingles, most advertisers will want to offer you a "buy-out" deal, in which they'd pay you a flat fee for the use of your song and then they'd own it from then on. You wouldn't receive any further royalties, even if it ran on the air for fifteen years. Remember the commercial for "Life" cereal, the one in which "Mikey liked it"? I believe it was on the air for sixteen years. Imagine how awful you'd feel if you'd signed a buy-out deal on that one. So if someone wants to buy you out, what you have to do is politely turn that down and suggest instead you'll allow them to *use* or license the song for a year for a specified amount of money. If they want to use it for succeeding years, they'll have to pay you another lump sum at the beginning of each new term. That protects both of you. The jingle company doesn't have to put out a huge amount of money in the short run and you will have some income protection for the future. Plus—and this is a big plus—when your jingles are performed you should receive what is known as "small performances" on them. Here's how that works.

Whenever a song is performed for profit, it earns money. The performing rights societies, ASCAP, BMI and SESAC, constantly survey radio stations, TV stations, cable stations, and Muzak for all pieces of music played on the air. Each radio and TV station has to purchase an annual license to air copyrighted material and songwriters are paid quarterly. In order to determine which songs are played during that year, the performing rights societies survey the stations for all performances for profit. Jingles are included in this category but are paid at a much smaller royalty rate than regular songs. If you have a jingle that's played a lot, however, those small performances can add up. Always include them when negotiating a contract for a jingle. They are payable to both the writer and the publisher of the jingle, so the sums we're discussing here are considerable. Whatever you do, don't let some fast-talking guy who works out of the trunk of his stolen car schmooze you out of your small performances. If you don't get them, he will, under the guise of being the publisher of the jingle. Let him be publisher, but don't let him collect your small performance royalties as a writer, too.

Developing writers may argue with me by saying that you have to let one go to get something else. But look at it this way. What if the stars have determined you will have this one jingle and it'll be your only source of income for the next twenty years until you have that long-awaited smash? Then how stupid and abused will you feel if you didn't demand the small performances that are legally yours? They aren't paid by the jingle company, but by the radio station. So demand them. And get them.

NO UNION PROTECTION

What's always been interesting to me is that when commercials are performed, the arranger automatically gets royalties. So does every singer and musician. But there is no songwriters' or jingle writers' union, so it's still dog-eat-dog out there. I'm hoping that by reading this chapter and referring to it again and again, you will not be robbed of royalties and income that is rightfully yours.

SINGING TELEGRAMS

In addition to jingle writing, compose original material for a singing-telegram company. You also might get to deliver the telegram, so you can sharpen your performance skills, too. And you never know who's going to be present when you show up. Trust that you'll get your big break somewhere and your job is simply to explore all avenues.

GOSPEL

If you're of the faith, try writing contemporary Christian music. That's a hidden market, and there is a fortune to be made in it. The songs on Christian stations follow all the rules of craft necessary in pop songs. They simply have a different lyrical message. Occasionally a contemporary Christian artist will "cross over" onto the pop charts. This happened with Amy Grant. Her last album went gold. And right afterward, she had enough clout to record a *pop* duet with Peter Cetera, called "Next Time I Fall," that also went gold and established her as a pop artist.

CUSTOM-TAILORED TUNES

Write personalized limericks or sonnets and set them to music for weddings, birthdays, anniversaries, graduations, Mother's Day, Father's Day, Valentine's Day and Christmas. Gain a reputation for being clever, accommodating, getting the job done on time and pleasing the client. That will help you in your other pursuits, because while you're doing this alternative line of work only until you can write songs full time, so are most of the people you come in contact with along the way. You never know whether the receptionist at the Gorilla Gram company will become president of PolyGram someday. People are more apt to do business with someone they already know and with whom they've had success in the past. Move up together. Make that your motto.

COPYWRITING

If you're a lyricist and can't write music, be a copywriter. They use related skills. Selling a product and selling a song are the same. The tag lines used in advertising are like song titles—short and snappy. You'll be earning money as a writer, not a waiter, and you'll be working with creative people. Who knows? Maybe the agency employing you will need a jingle at some point.

That happened to a copywriter on the Kodak account. His company hired Roger Nichols, composer of "We've Only Just Begun" and "I Won't Last A Day Without You," to write a melody for a new Kodak campaign. The copywriter, who to the best of my knowledge had never had a hit song before, was there at the right time and did the lyric for "Good Morning Yesterday," which turned into a commercial and later a smash hit for Paul Anka.

TEACH

If you're more musically than lyrically oriented, teach music—guitar, piano or voice. You'll be earning a living, working "in the business," and you never know who will walk through your door.

HIRE A LAWYER

Most creative people are terrible negotiators. They can't separate themselves from the product they're selling. I would strongly recommend you always have someone else do your deal-making for you, just as you would when negotiating a publishing contract.

Never trust verbal agreements. Always get it in writing. If a guy won't sign an agreement, he won't pay you either. So always, always insist on a contract. And hire a lawyer to handle it for you.

While you're exploring alternative sources of income within the writing and music fields, you're sharpening your writing skills. You're learning to tailor your songs to specific requirements, which is what you must do when writing for a particular artist. Who knows when you'll bump into someone during your scuffling days who wants a real song? If you're used to writing on assignment, you'll be ready for anything and will do a terrific job. Satisfied customers will come back to you for more. What you're doing here is taking charge of your life, creating a cash flow and gaining confidence as a writer. That last item, confidence, is the most important ingredient you have for sale, both to yourself and to prospective customers.

SEASONS

It's essential for all songwriters to remember that even the most successful of their heroes and colleagues have suffered enormous defeats, setbacks and failures. But they bounced back.

I've had publishers throw me out of their offices, tossing my demos after me and yelling, "Gimme somethin' I can dance to." And just a few months later those same songs got standing ovations at Carnegie Hall. So who's right? The insensitive publisher or the appreciative audience in New York?

Oscar Hammerstein II and Jerome Kern wrote splendidly together. When that collaboration ended, Hammerstein suffered ten years of desperate nothing until his next hit broke through. And what a hit it was! *Oklahoma!*, written with Richard Rogers, set that team in motion and they never looked back.

It's important to remember that each of us has his own timetable. If you think all the rocks stars are twenty-two, look again. I've known demo singers who were thirty-three when they worked for me ten years ago. Now they're rock stars and they're only thirty-four. Maybe the road has done strange things to their left brain cells. Somebody's rewriting birth certificates. I've never known anyone in the music business over thirty who didn't deduct five years from how old he is. So don't be intimidated by rock stars' youthful ages. They're probably grandparents.

Hal David was forty before he had his first hit. That in itself was frustrating, but add to it the fact that his older brother, Mack, was one of the most successful lyricists in the world and had *his* first hit at nineteen. Think what Hal was up against. Imagine, though, how hard he had to fight to stay in the game. He stuck it out, hung in there, teamed up with Burt Bacharach, and eventually surpassed the success of everyone who was in line ahead of him, including his brother.

Even Bacharach has had his slumps. After his partnership with Hal David ended, he seemed to disappear. His old songs, of course, were everywhere, but it took ten years for him to get back on the charts with "Arthur's Theme"—which won an Oscar. Look at him now. He had two Number One hits in the same year—"That's What Friends Are For" and "On My Own." How's that for bouncing back?

What about Kenny Rogers? He began with the New Christy Minstrels. After they had their time in the sun, they faded. Several years went by and Kenny reappeared with another group, the First Edition, and stayed on the charts another couple of years. Their biggest hit, "Ruby, Don't Take Your Love to Town," was written during the Korean War, but wasn't recorded until the Vietnam War. Talk about a song having to wait its turn. Anyway, as will happen to most artists and groups, the First Edition faded. Kenny was gone for eight more years. I mean *gone*. He didn't even have a label deal. Same voice. Same track record. No deal.

In 1975, an Australian singer/stripper I knew who was down on her luck lived next door to a guy she said "used to be Kenny Rogers." Kenny, who incidentally was still Kenny, lived in a furnished single in the Valley. The Australian and everyone else in the world thought Kenny was washed up. Forgotten. History.

But Kenny didn't think so. Out of left field, Larry Butler, who was on a roll at the time as a country producer, cut three sides with him. One of the songs, "Love Lifted Me," which was more gospel than country, caught the attention of the executives at United Artists. The single was released and got Kenny back on the charts. Not long after, beaming Larry played me a song he'd just cut with Kenny called "Lucille." You know the rest. Kenny had a brand-new career. He's never done better in his life. And those white hairs aren't makeup either.

As for the Australian singer/stripper, the last I heard she was still in the same dump in the Valley. Kenny, on the other hand, bought a home in Bel Air for $14 million cash, the amount he'd been guaranteed in concert dates just for that year alone.

When I met Kim Carnes, she was a demo singer. She'd made three solo albums that failed. But she kept on singing. She did demos for $25 for all the top writers in town. I frankly think I got most of my records because the artists hoped they'd sound as good as Kim did singing my songs. And while many other demo singers I knew often had chips on their shoulders, resenting the fact that they weren't going to be the final artists on particular tracks (and calling in sick with mysterious diseases of the throat ten minutes before the session or making me go get them from their flea traps in Venice and personally deliver them to the studio in my VW), Kim drove her own Mercedes to work and couldn't have been easier to deal with. Aside from having the world's best voice, which made my songs sound better than I ever dreamed they were, she was on time, she would phrase lyrics exactly the way I asked her to and she'd get the song down quickly, usually on the first take. She even did the background parts without any extra pay or prodding. Kim was a professional. She knew if she just hung in there, her time would come. Five years later, it did. She won a Grammy for "Bette Davis Eyes," the Record of the Year.

Tom Snow, composer of "You Should Hear How She Talks about You," "He's So Shy" and "Let's Hear It for the Boy," had nothing to show for his first seven years in the business except an annual income of $1,500—less than what families in Appalachia were earning. Tom recorded two solo albums, one of which took seven months to complete. They both stiffed. But soon afterward he met and collaborated with Leo Sayer. Then he was rolling. The only thing that got him through the agony that preceded his success was his unrelenting belief in himself. He remembered that only *one* of Vincent van Gogh's paintings was sold during his lifetime. Now we're lined up three deep in 99° weather waiting to see them on their rare visits to museums. If Van Gogh or Oscar Hammerstein or Kenny Rogers or Kim Carnes or Tom Snow believed they were only good when other people said they were, the world would be suffering from great artistic poverty. If you're good, know it, even if nobody else does. You write and you rewrite. You keep going. Don't let anybody or anything get in your way.

All of my colleagues—*your* colleagues—have stories like these. The bottom line is persistence. If you don't give up, your time will come. A writer's job is to write. If you write well and pursue originality and perfection, the world will know your work. But until then, you must feel in your soul that you've got the greatness and the magic to go the distance. No gold record, no Grammy can give you that. You have to give it to yourself. Every day. All day. For the rest of your life.

People get hot and cold. When you get hot, it's because you created the heat. When you're cold, don't fall into the trap of thinking somebody took something away from you. I have colleagues who've gone from a Mercedes to a moped and back to a Mercedes again. Some are hitchhiking in Gucci shoes. We don't live in straight lines. We zigzag. Andy Warhol claimed we each get fifteen minutes in the spotlight. While I disagree with his timetable, I do concur that we don't get lucky and stay hot forever. It's a roller coaster called "the music business." If you want to ride along with us, buy your ticket and be prepared. Just remember when you're in a slump, it is only temporary. If George Burns and Tina Turner can come back, so can you.

Write well. Surprise me. Dazzle me. I'm counting on it. You are the future of music. The world needs your songs. Please—don't let us down.

AUDIO TAPES BY MOLLY-ANN LEIKIN

1. "The Songwriter's Success Series" parts 1, 2, 3, 4.

Nurturing, motivating, funny, 3-1/2 hours:

How to get ready to write • How to write love songs that say something new • How to write great opening lines • The power of rewriting • How to avoid synthesizer dependency • The value of visual writing • What to do if your father thinks you're a bum • How to make deadlines work for you • How to make yourself famous • Dealing with completion anxiety • Homework for the mind • Hustling - nicely • Ethics • The fast buck got stuck in traffic • Packaging = power • Facing the past • The pleasures of pain • Eavesdropping • How to make your network work for you

2. "How To Write A Hit Song And Live To Hear It On The Air"

Practical, concise, witty, 3-1/2 hours:

Structure • Coping with rejection • Making terrific, low cost demos • Overcoming writing blocks • Marketing your songs • Making money in the meantime • Collaborating • Making time to write

Make your check or money order payable to Songwriting Consultants Ltd., 2118 Wilshire Blvd. #882, Santa Monica, CA 90403.

1. **The Songwriter's Success Series**
  $49.95 & $3.50 postage and 8.5% CA sales tax = $57.94
2. **How To Write A Hit Song And Live To Hear It On The Air**
  $49.95 & $3.50 postage and 8.5% CA sales tax = $57.94

Name_____

Address_____

City/State_____Zip_____

Day Phone (___)_____Evening Phone(___)_____

VISA/MC#_____Exp. Date_____

If you would like information on how to schedule a private consultation with Molly-Ann Leikin or one of her associates, by phone, fax, through the mail or in person, to evaluate your material and help you develop a marketing plan for it, check here (   ).